Time for French

All it takes is twenty minutes a day

Paul Durrant

Stanley Thornes (Publishers) Ltd

First published in 1999 by:
Stanley Thornes (Publishers) Ltd
Ellenborough House
Wellington Street
CHELTENHAM GL50 1YW
England

A catalogue record for this book is available
from the British Library.

99 00 01 02 03 / 10 9 8 7 6 5 4 3 2 1

ISBN 0–7487–3872–X (book)
ISBN 0–7487–3874–6 (complete pack)
ISBN 0–7487–3873–8 (cassettes)

Also available in the *Time for Languages* series:

Time for German, Corinna Schicker
Time for Italian, Donatella de Ferra, Marina Mozzon-McPherson
Time for Portuguese, Sue Tyson-Ward
Time for Spanish, Robert Clarke

Cover: Joanna Kerr

Typeset by Action Publishing Technology Limited, Gloucester
Recorded at Matinée Sound & Vision, Reading
Voice artists: Bénédicte Paviot, Olivier Jacoulet, Corinne Amoros
Printed and bound in Great Britain by T. J. International Ltd, Padstow, Cornwall

How to make the best use of *Time for French*

The material in *Time for French* has been designed for you to complete one unit every day, but you are in control. If you want to cover several units in a day, then do that. Do try, however, to stick to a sensible routine so that you cover a number of units spread over the course of one week, rather than ten sessions at the week-end. You will retain so much more if you 'drip-feed' yourself. You should ideally work through the units in sequence, but again, you are in control. Choose a method which suits you best.

Start each unit by listening carefully to the pronunciation in the **Vocabulary** section on your cassette and repeat in the gaps provided. Take full advantage of this facility, which is provided until unit 30.

Next listen twice to the **Dialogue** section, first without using your book, then a second time, referring to the written text.

When you are ready, work through the exercises (**Ecoutez!; Lisez!/Ecrivez!; Et parlez français!**). Some of these involve using the cassette, some don't. In the exercise **Et parlez français!**, you will be asked to take part in a speaking activity with an actor on the cassette. Usually there will be prompts in English on the record-ing or written or in picture form in the book, and gaps for you to speak. You will soon get used to the method used here, and you will find it invaluable in gaining the con-fidence to speak in natural situations.

Refer to the **En français** (language notes) as you work and the background infor-mation on France in the **En France** section at the end of each unit.

Make a habit of referring back to **cross-referenced units** in the same Activity Area which you have already covered. These unit numbers appear at the top of each right-hand page from unit 14.

Finally, don't be shy! Anywhere is a good place to listen and speak – in bed, in the car, doing the ironing or whatever, so Bonne chance! – Good luck! Now it's **Time for French!**

Contents

Greetings and introductions

First meetings

Vocabulaire (Vocabulary)

Bonjour!	Good morning/afternoon!		
Bonsoir!	Good evening!		
Au revoir!	Goodbye!		
monsieur	sir, Mr	**français**	French
madame	madam, Mrs	**anglais**	English
mademoiselle	miss	**américain**	American
		italien	Italian
je suis	I am		
vous êtes	you are	**de Londres**	from London
oui	yes	**en vacances**	on holiday
non	no		

Dialogues

Marie Simon	Bonjour, monsieur.
Roland Baral	Bonjour, madame.
Anne Simon	Bonsoir, monsieur.
Roland Baral	Bonsoir, mademoiselle.
Marie Simon	Vous êtes français?
Roland Baral	Oui, je suis français.
Roland Baral	Vous êtes anglaise?
Tracey Smith	Oui, je suis anglaise.
Roland Baral	Vous êtes de Londres?
Tracey Smith	Oui, je suis de Londres.
Anne Simon	Vous êtes de Paris?
Roland Baral	Oui, je suis de Paris.
Roland Baral	Vous êtes en vacances?
Tracey Smith	Oui, je suis en vacances.
Anne Simon	Vous êtes anglais, monsieur?
Marco Rossi	Non, je suis italien.
	Je suis de Rome.
Roland Baral	Vous êtes française, madame?
Steffi Woods	Non, je suis américaine.
	Je suis de New York.
Anne Simon	Au revoir, monsieur!
Roland Baral	Au revoir, madame!
	Au revoir, mademoiselle!

1 Ecoutez! (Listen!)
Listen to the conversation on your recording and tick the boxes **VRAI** (true) or **FAUX** (false). (*Answers on page 126.*)

	VRAI	FAUX
a) The conversation takes place in the morning		
b) The woman is French		
c) The woman is from Bordeaux		
d) The man is English		
e) The man is from Liverpool		
f) The woman is on holiday		

2 Lisez! Ecrivez! (Read! Write!)
Fill in the missing letters. (*Answers on page 126.*)

B _ _ s _ _ r   Je s _ _ _   L _ _ d _ _ s
m _ _ s _ _ _ r   V _ _ _ ê _ _ s   fr _ _ ç _ _ s

3 ... et parlez français! (and speak French!)
What would these people say about themselves? Think what they would say first, have a go yourself and then listen to the recording to check you were correct. The first one has been written out for you. (*Answers on page 126.*)

Je suis français. _____   _____   _____
Je suis de Paris. _____   _____   _____

En français (In French)

In French all *nouns*, whether they refer to people or to things, are either *masculine* or *feminine*. If an adjective, like **anglais**, **français**, **américain**, is used to describe a feminine noun it is written with an **e** to 'agree'.

> **Vous êtes français, monsieur?**
> **Vous êtes française, madame?**

Note: Only the *masculine* form appears in the vocabulary.

En France (In France)

When greeting each other formally the French add **monsieur**, **madame** or, for a girl or young woman, **mademoiselle**. (There is, as yet, no French equivalent of 'Ms'.) Note that **Bonsoir** is used both as a greeting and when saying goodbye in the evening.

2 In the café
Ordering drinks

Vocabulaire (Vocabulary)

Messieurs-dames	Ladies and gentlemen
vous désirez?	What would you like?
un café	a café *or* a coffee
un kir	a white wine with blackcurrant liqueur
une orange pressée	a freshly squeezed orange juice
et une bière	and a beer
pression	draught (beer)
bouteille	bottle
deux crèmes	two white coffees
trois cocas	three coca-colas
s'il vous plaît	please
tout de suite	right away, immediately
merci	thank you
ou	or
alors	so, let's see

Dialogues

1. Waiter — Messieurs-dames, bonjour.
Vous désirez?
Marie — Deux crèmes, s'il vous plaît.
Waiter — Deux crèmes? Tout de suite.

2. Customer — Mademoiselle!
Waitress — Oui, monsieur. Tout de suite.
Vous désirez?
Customer — Alors, une orange pressée, un kir, trois cocas, et une bière, s'il vous plaît.
Waitress — Une orange pressée, un kir, trois cocas, et une bière. Pression ou bouteille?
Customer — Pression, s'il vous plaît.
Waitress — Merci.

Exercices (Exercises)

1 Ecoutez! (Listen!)
Listen to the recording and tick each drink when you hear it mentioned. One of these is *not* mentioned – which one? (*Answer on page 126*).

black coffee	____
white coffee	____
beer	____
kir	____
orange juice	____
coca-cola	____

2 Lisez! Ecrivez! (Read! Write!)
Fill in the orders, using the text opposite to help you. (*Answers on page 126.*)
U _ _ _ _ é.   U _ _   _ _ _ _ e .   D _ _ x c _ c _ s.
U _ k _ r.   T _ _ _ s o _ _ _ _ _ s p _ _ _ _ _ s.

3 ... et parlez français! (and speak French!)
Re-create the café dialogue on the facing page using the details below and
speaking in the pauses on the recording. (*Answers on page 126.*)

a)   b)

En français (In French)

Just as the masculine adjective changes to agree with a feminine noun (Unit 1), so
there is a masculine and a feminine form, **un** and **une**, for the English 'a'.

Masculine nouns	***un* garçon**	a waiter
	***un* café**	a coffee
Feminine nouns	***une* serveuse**	a waitress
	***une* bière**	a beer

Note: **un** and **une** are also used to mean 'one'.

un coca one coca-cola	**une bière** one beer

En France (In France)

You can find a **café, bar** or **bistro** on almost every street corner in the centre of a
French town. In fine weather they spill over on to the pavement where prices are
usually slightly more – **à la terrasse** (on the terrace) – than if you stand at the
counter. If your drinks are brought to you, pay the waiter (**le garçon**) or waitress
(**la serveuse**). If you drink at the counter then you pay **à la caisse** (at the till). A
tip (**un pourboire**) is optional, but usually service is included (**service compris**)
in the bill.

3 At the hotel

Checking in

 Vocabulaire (Vocabulary)

vous avez	you have
une chambre	a room
libre	free
pour	for
combien de personnes?	how many people?
une nuit	1 night
deux personnes	2 people
trois cents francs	300 francs
numéro quatre	number 4
avec bain	with bath
avec douche	with shower
la clé	the key
Ça va?	Is that all right?
très bien	very good, that's fine
voilà	there you are

 Dialogue

Customer	Bonsoir.
Receptionist	Bonsoir, monsieur.
Customer	Vous avez une chambre libre?
Receptionist	Oui. Pour combien de personnes?
Customer	Pour deux personnes.
Receptionist	Avec bain?
Customer	Avec douche.
Receptionist	Pour combien de nuits?
Customer	Une nuit.
Receptionist	Très bien. Trois cents francs. Ça va?
Customer	Très bien.
Receptionist	Alors chambre numéro quatre.
	Voilà la clé, monsieur.
Customer	Merci.

Exercices (Exercises)

1 Ecoutez! (Listen!)

On your recording three people are booking hotel rooms. Fill in the grid below according to their requirements. (*Answers on page 126*.)

Customer	Single/double	Bath/shower	No. of nights	Room no.
1				
2				
3				

2 Ecrivez! (Write!)

Complete the sentence using the pictures as clues. (*Answers on page 126.*)

Vous avez une _ _ _ _ _ _ _ pour trois _ _ _ _ _ pour _ _ _ _
personnes avec _ _ _ _ _ _ _ , s'il vous _ _ _ _ _?

3 … et parlez français! (and speak French!)

Re-create the dialogue on the facing page using the following change of
details. (*Answers on page 126.*)

a)

b)

En français (In French)

As in English, most French nouns form their plural by adding **s**.

une nuit	one night	**deux nuits**	two nights

In French, however, final consonants of words are usually *not* pronounced. Check
the dialogue again for the pronunciation of **deu̱x personne̱s, troi̱s cenṯs**.

En France (In France)

French hotels are good value with prices per room rather than per person.
Recent expansion of cheap hotel chains catering for the motorway traveller has
brought prices down still further. Away from the motorways and airports you will
still find the old-style **auberge** (inn or country hotel) and the family-run **pension**
(hotel or guest house), often categorised from one to four stars (**étoiles**). Note
that breakfast is usually **non compris** (not included) in the price of the room.

Numbers

Asking the time

 Vocabulaire

un	1	onze	11	vingt et un	21
deux	2	douze	12	vingt-deux	22
trois	3	treize	13	vingt-trois	23
quatre	4	quatorze	14	vingt-quatre	24
cinq	5	quinze	15	vingt-cinq	25
six	6	seize	16	vingt-six	26
sept	7	dix-sept	17	vingt-sept	27
huit	8	dix-huit	18	vingt-huit	28
neuf	9	dix-neuf	19	vingt-neuf	29
dix	10	vingt	20		

heure	hour, time
Quelle heure est-il?	What time is it?
Il est …	It is …
une heure	one o'clock
deux heures	two o'clock
midi	midday
minuit	midnight
huit heures dix	ten past eight
neuf heures et quart	quarter past nine
dix heures et demie	half past ten
onze heures moins le quart	quarter to eleven (lit. less the quarter)

Dialogues

Quelle heure est-il?

a)
Il est une heure

b)
Il est deux heures

c)
Il est quatre heures cinq

d)
Il est six heures et quart

e)
Il est huit heures vingt-cinq

f)
Il est neuf heures et demie

g)
Il est dix heures moins le quart

h)
Il est onze heures moins dix

i)
Il est midi   Il est minuit

Exercices

1 Ecoutez!

Listen again to the numbers 1–29 at the start of this unit and practise counting until you are familiar with them. Then try exercises a) and b). (*Answers on page 126.*)

a) Write down the following numbers as you hear them. The first is done for you.

11 __ __ __ __ __ __

b) **Quelle heure est-il?** Now listen to these times and draw in the hands on the clocks.

2 Lisez!

Refer first to **En français**, section 3. Then write the following times in figures as in the examples. (*Answers on page 126.*)

Trois heures et demie	3h30	d) Quatre heures et quart	___
a) Deux heures douze	___	e) Neuf heures quatorze	___
b) Six heures vingt-deux	___	f) Sept heures moins le quart	___
c) Neuf heures cinq	___	g) Onze heures moins dix	___

3 ... et parlez français!

Refer to the **En français** (Pronunciation) section, then answer the question **Quelle heure est-il?** using these times. (*Answers on page 126.*)

a) 3.00   b) 7.00   c) 12.00 (midday)   d) 8.25   e) 11.15

En français

1. *Pronunciation.* Final consonants are normally silent in French. But notice on your recording that the final consonant of numbers 5–10 is often pronounced, and always when counting, at the end of a phrase or before the **h** in **heures**.

numéro huit   **onze heures moins dix**   **six heures**

2. The French for 21 is **vingt et un** – 'twenty and one'.

3. When writing times in figures, **heures** is abbreviated to **h**. e.g. **22h15** – 22.15 (10.15 p.m.).

En France

The 24-hour clock is always used in France for timetables and public announcements, so be prepared to hear, for example, **quatorze heures** or **vingt-deux heures quinze** in stations and airports rather than **deux heures** and **dix heures et quart**.

Talking about yourself

Saying where you are from

Vocabulaire

je travaille	I work
je parle	I speak
j'habite	I live
je m'appelle	my name is (lit. I call myself)
je viens	I come
nous habitons	we live
vous parlez	you speak
vous venez	you come
à Londres	in London
mais	but
assez bien	quite well
ma femme	my wife
mon mari	my husband
la famille	the family

Dialogue

Claire Forrestier	Vous êtes de Londres?
Peter Jones	Non, je travaille à Londres, mais j'habite à Bedford.
Claire Forrestier	Vous parlez très bien français.
Peter Jones	Assez bien. Ma femme est française, et je parle français avec la famille. Et vous, madame, vous venez de Paris?
Claire Forrestier	Non, je viens de Nice mais mon mari est parisien et nous habitons à Paris.
Peter Jones	Ah, voilà ma femme, Chantal.

Exercices

1 Ecoutez!

Listen to four people talking about themselves and supply the missing information. (*Answers on page 126.*)

Surname	First Name	Nationality	Comes from	Lives in	Works in
	Alan		London		
Bouchet			Paris	Cannes	Nice
	John	American			
Dupont				Lyon	Grenoble

2   Lisez! Ecrivez!
Rearrange these jumbled sentences. (*Answers on page 126.*)

a) très   monsieur   parlez   bien   Vous   français
b) Paris   venez   de   Vous?
c) avec   français   Je   famille   la   parle
d) Nice   viens   Je   mais   est   de   parisien   mari   mon

3   ... et parlez français!

Play the dialogue again. Stop the recording as necessary and take the part of Claire Forrestier. Check your answers on the recording.
1.   Start by asking Peter Jones if he is from London.
2.   When he answers, say that he speaks French very well.
3.   He asks if you come from Paris. Answer no, and add that you come from Nice but that your husband is Parisian and you both live in Paris.

En français

1. *Verbs*. Note how the end of a verb changes according to who performs the action, i.e. whether it is 'I', for example, or 'we' or 'you'. Listen and watch out for the different forms.

I	we	you
Je parl<u>e</u>	**Nous parl<u>ons</u>**	**Vous parl<u>ez</u>**
J'habit<u>e</u>	**Nous habit<u>ons</u>**	**Vous habit<u>ez</u>**

Make an effort to learn by heart those commonly used *irregular* verbs which do not follow this pattern, e.g. **je suis**, **je viens**. They will be introduced gradually during the course and you will find them together in the Verb Tables on pages 131–2.

2. The French for 'my' is **mon**. This is the form to use with a masculine noun. The feminine is **ma**.

mon mari (masculine) my husband	**ma femme** (feminine) my wife

The plural is **mes**, e.g. **mes clés** 'my keys'.

En France

When two French people meet for the first time they say **enchanté** (written **enchantée** if it is a woman speaking). This is short for **enchanté(e) de faire votre connaissance**. (Note that only the masculine form is given in the vocabulary.) The literal meaning is 'Enchanted to make your acquaintance'. More informally, and especially with young people, the normal thing to do is just to say your name and shake hands.

6 Out and about

Asking for directions

 Vocabulaire

Pardon	Excuse me
Est-ce qu'il y a	Is there
une banque	a bank
près d'ici	near here
C'est	It's
assez	quite
loin d'ici	far from here
à pied	on foot
en voiture	in a car, by car
vous allez	you go
vous tournez	you turn
j'ai	I have
tout droit	straight on
à gauche	on the left
à droite	on the right
jusqu'à l'hôtel	(until you get) to the hotel
la deuxième rue	the second street

 Dialogue

Tourist	Pardon, madame.
	Est-ce qu'il y a une banque près d'ici?
Passer-by	Oui, monsieur. Vous avez la Banque Nationale de Paris et le Crédit Lyonnais. Vous êtes à pied ou en voiture?
Tourist	J'ai la voiture, mais … c'est loin d'ici?
Passer-by	Alors, le Crédit Lyonnais est assez loin. Pour la BNP vous allez tout droit jusqu'à l'Hôtel de Paris. Vous tournez à gauche et c'est la deuxième rue à droite.
Tourist	Merci, madame.

Exercices

1 **Lisez!**

Read these three sets of directions and follow them on the map opposite, starting at the arrow. Where do you finish up in each case?

A "Allez jusqu'à la banque. Tournez à droite et c'est la deuxième rue à droite."

B "Vous allez tout droit et vous tournez à gauche."

C "Vous tournez à gauche, vous allez tout droit et c'est la deuxième rue à gauche." (*Answers on page 126.*)

Answers: A . . . .

                B . . . .

                C . . . .

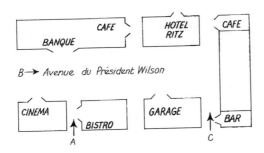

B→ Avenue du Président Wilson

2 Lisez!

Match the halves of these sentences. (*Answers on page 126.*)

a) Le Crédit Lyonnais
b) Vous allez
c) Vous êtes
d) Vous tournez
e) Est-ce qu'il y a

i) tout droit
ii) une banque près d'ici?
iii) est assez loin d'ici
iv) à pied ou en voiture?
v) à gauche

3 … et parlez français!

Re-create the dialogue. Play the part of the tourist looking for a restaurant.
(*Answers on page 126.*)

En français

1. In Unit 2 you saw that French has two words for the indefinite article 'a'. There are also two words in French for the definite article 'the' – **le** and **la**.

Masculine **le bar** the bar	*Feminine* **la rue** the street.

2. **Le** and **la** both change to **l'** before a word beginning with a vowel or silent **h** (**h** is not usually pronounced in French).

l'heure the hour	**l'orange** the orange

3. You can ask 'Is there a bank?' by saying either **Est-ce qu'il y a une banque?** or simply raising your voice at the end of the phrase – **Il y a une banque?**

4. **J'ai** – 'I have', **vous avez** – 'you have'. These are two of the forms of the common irregular verb **avoir** – 'to have'.

5. Note the spelling and pronunciation of **tout droit** (**t** silent) and **à droite** (**t** pronounced).

En France

To attract someone's attention the French say **Pardon** or **Excusez-moi!** Whichever you use, remember always to follow with **monsieur, madame** or **mademoiselle**. If someone has been particularly helpful you can say **Merci beaucoup** or **Vous êtes très gentil** (kind), **monsieur** or **Vous êtes très gentille, madame/mademoiselle.**

Public transport

Buying a train ticket

Vocabulaire

je voudrais	I would like
deux billets	two tickets
aller simple	single
aller-retour	return
trois cent vingt	three hundred and twenty
le prochain train	the next train
part	departs
arrive	arrives
à quelle heure?	at what time?
C'est direct?	Is it direct?
quai numéro quatre	platform number four
merci beaucoup	thank you very much
Je vous en prie	Not at all, don't mention it.

Dialogue

Ticket clerk	Monsieur?
Roland Baral	Je voudrais deux billets pour Nantes, s'il vous plaît.
Ticket clerk	Aller simple ou aller-retour?
Roland Baral	Aller-retour.
Ticket clerk	Trois cent vingt francs, s'il vous plaît.
Roland Baral	Le prochain train part à quelle heure?
Ticket clerk	A treize heures dix, monsieur. Quai numéro quatre.
Roland Baral	Et il arrive à Nantes à quelle heure, s'il vous plaît?
Ticket clerk	A quinze heures dix-sept.
Roland Baral	C'est direct?
Ticket clerk	Oui, oui, c'est direct.
Roland Baral	Merci beaucoup, madame.
Ticket clerk	Je vous en prie, monsieur.

```
SNCF        BILLET   [ BESANCON VIOTTE   → PARIS GARE LYON
            Valable 24 heures maximum après compostage
                                          01ADULTE

Dep 02/04 à 07H00 de BESANCON VIOTTE   Classe 2  VOIT 15: PLACE NO  22
Arr       à 09H34 à PARIS GARE LYON    01ASSIS FUMEUR
A UTILISER DANS LE TRAIN    774 TGV    SALLE         01COULOIR
TARIF CARRISSIMO

Dep    à      de ***                   Classe *
Arr    à      à

Prix par voyageur :  125.00                         [ Prix FRF   **125.00 ]
CJ45 PC 50 KM0406        :              :OV 712919933  BESANCON VIOTTE
  125      243           :              :CA    0  010496  12H02
BD NIV.1  877129199338                  :S012AC Dossier :  RRFJDD    Page 1/1
          473863829
```

Exercices

1 Ecoutez!
Listen to the booking clerk as he issues rail tickets and fill in the missing details. (*Answers on page 126.*)

Destination	Single/Return	Departure	Arrival	Platform	Price
a) Nice		09h10		7	220F
b)	aller-retour		17h20		
c) Marseille		06h07			

2 Lisez! Ecrivez!
Rearrange these jumbled sentences. (*Answers on page 126.*)
a) simple voudrais Je un pour aller Paris.
b) quelle s'il heure arrive vous Il plaît à?
c) prie monsieur vous en Je.
d) train part quelle Le à heure prochain?

3 … et parlez français!
Re-create the dialogue at the station ticket office. Use the prompts on your recording, and make a note of the price, times and platform number. (*Answers on page 126.*)

En français

1. In the dialogue the train is referred to not as 'it' but as 'he' – **il**, since **train** is a masculine noun. **Il arrive à quelle heure?** So **il arrive** can mean either 'he arrives' or 'it arrives'. Similarly, **elle** can mean either 'she' or 'it'.

2. *The present tense.* When you look up a verb in the dictionary you will be given the *infinitive*, e.g. **parler** for 'to speak', and you must replace the **-er** with the ending you need for **je**, **nous** etc., in order to use the verb to talk about present events. Note that the ending **-e** is used for **il/elle** as well as for **je**.

je parl<u>e</u>	je travaill<u>e</u>	j'arriv<u>e</u>
il/elle parl<u>e</u>	il/elle travaill<u>e</u>	il/elle arriv<u>e</u>

Remember most *regular* **-ER** verbs follow this pattern.

En France

Notice the 24-hour clock is used in the dialogue for train times. Once inside the **gare SNCF (Société Nationale des Chemins de Fer Français)** look out for signs saying **RENSEIGNEMENTS** (information), **GUICHET** (ticket office), **COR-RESPONDANCES** (connections) and **HORAIRE** (timetable) giving **DEPARTS** (departures) and **ARRIVEES** (arrivals). A machine with the words **Compostez votre billet** tells you to punch your ticket before boarding the train. Finally, the French for 'Have a good journey!' – **Bon voyage!**

8 Shopping

At the market

Vocabulaire

Donnez-moi	Give me
3F 60 la pièce	3F 60 each
et puis	and then
Et avec ça?	Anything else?
une douzaine	a dozen
un kilo	a kilo
grammes	grams
olives vertes	green olives
œufs	eggs
artichauts	artichokes
tomates	tomatoes
ça fait	that makes
C'est tout	That's all
Bonne journée!	Have a good day!
trente	thirty
trente et un	thirty-one
quarante	forty
quarante et un	forty-one
cinquante	fifty
soixante	sixty

Dialogue

Trader	Madame?
Customer	Je voudrais un kilo de tomates, s'il vous plaît.
Trader	Voilà, madame. Huit francs quarante. Et avec ça?
Customer	C'est combien, les artichauts?
Trader	Trois francs soixante la pièce, madame.
Customer	Alors donnez-moi trois artichauts, s'il vous plaît. Et puis cent cinquante grammes d'olives vertes et une douzaine d'œufs, s'il vous plaît.
Trader	Voilà … C'est tout, madame?
Customer	Oui, merci.
Trader	Alors, ça fait quarante et un francs soixante, s'il vous plaît, madame … Cinquante francs, merci. Et voilà huit francs quarante. Merci, madame. Bonne journée.
Customer	Merci. Au revoir, monsieur.

Exercices

1 Ecoutez!

Listen to these items from a shopping list and write down the amount and the price of each item. (*Answers on page 126.*)

_____ de bananes? _____ F _____ , s'il vous plaît.

_____ d'olives? _____ F _____ , s'il vous plaît.

_____ d'œufs? _____ F _____ , s'il vous plaît.

2 Ecrivez!

Complete the crossword, then arrange the words to make a sentence which you might overhear in the market. Just one clue – the first word is **Je**. (*Answers on page 126.*)

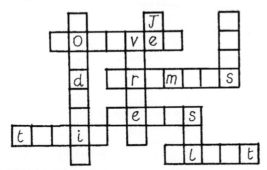

3 ... et parlez français!

You do some shopping at the market. Listen to the audio prompts and work out your total expenditure. (*Answers on page 126.*)

En français

1. The round numbers **trente, quarante, cinquante** and **soixante** are quite straightforward. Note that 31, 41, etc. are 'thirty and one', 'forty and one' – **trente et un, quarante et un.** Thereafter hyphens are used – **trente-deux, trente-trois,** etc.

2. *Expressions of quantity* are followed by **de** (**d'** before a vowel).

> **un kilo <u>de</u> tomates   une douzaine <u>d'</u>œufs   200 grammes <u>d'</u>olives**

3. Learn two ways of asking for things: **Je voudrais** – 'I would like' and **Donnez-moi ... s'il vous plaît** – 'Give me ... please'.

En France

Despite competition from the local **supermarché** (supermarket) and the out-of-town **hypermarché** (hypermarket), the traditional outdoor market – **le marché,** still thrives in France, providing the fresh, good quality produce so appreciated by French shoppers.

Services

At the tourist information office

 Vocabulaire

le syndicat d'initiative	the tourist information office
Je peux vous aider?	Can I help you?
bien sûr	of course
voici	here is
un plan de la ville	a street plan
Vous restez longtemps?	Are you staying long?
le programme des spectacles	the diary of events
jusqu'à	until
quelque chose	something
ce soir	this evening
concert folklorique	folk music concert
les enfants	the children
feux d'artifice	fireworks
marionnettes	puppets
intéressant	interesting
cirque national	national circus
prenez	take
gratuit	free

Les jours de la semaine	The days of the week
lundi	Monday
mardi	Tuesday
mercredi	Wednesday
jeudi	Thursday
vendredi	Friday
samedi	Saturday
dimanche	Sunday

 Dialogue

Employee	Je peux vous aider, monsieur?
Tourist	Oui, est-ce que vous avez un plan de Perpignan, s'il vous plaît?
Employee	Oui, bien sûr. Voici le plan de la ville. Vous restez longtemps à Perpignan, monsieur?
Tourist	Une semaine. Six jours jusqu'à samedi.
Employee	Alors j'ai le programme des spectacles jusqu'à vendredi. Voilà.
Tourist	Il y a quelque chose ce soir?
Employee	Ce soir à huit heures il y a un concert folklorique.
Tourist	Est-ce qu'il y a quelque chose pour les enfants?
Employee	Euh, voyons … mardi, feux d'artifice, mercredi, spectacle de marionnettes. C'est très intéressant pour les enfants. Puis jeudi, cirque national italien. Voilà, monsieur, prenez le programme, c'est gratuit.

Exercices

 1 **Ecoutez! Ecrivez!**
Listen to this recording of an information officer talking about local holiday events and fill in the missing details in the grid opposite. (*Answers on page 126.*)

Day	Time	Event
Monday	21.00	
		Fireworks
Friday		
		Italian National Circus

2   Lisez! Ecrivez!
Read the dialogue again, then from memory put the following into French for a postcard you are sending to a French friend. Start: **Je reste** … (*Answers on page 126.*)

a) I am staying in Nice until Friday   Je reste _____

_____

b) This evening there is a concert at seven o'clock _____

_____

c) Tuesday there is a circus for the children   _____

_____

d) Thursday there is a puppet show   _____

_____

3   … et parlez français!
Take the part of the tourists in the two scenes on your recording. (*Answers on page 126.*)

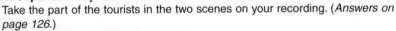

En français

The plural of definite articles **le** and **la** is **les**.

le jour	the day	**les jours**	the days
la semaine	the week	**les semaines**	the weeks

Remember that before a vowel both **le** and **la** change to **l'**.

l'enfant	the child

In the plural **l'** also changes to **les**.

les enfants	the children

En France

Information about **logement** (accommodation), **transports** and other tourist facilities as well as local attractions and entertainment (**spectacles** or **distractions**) can be found at the **Syndicat d'Initiative**, sometimes called the **Office de Tourisme**. You will find these in town centres and at motorway exits and as well as giving tourist information they will often be able to book your hotel for you.

Ordering lunch

Vocabulaire

Vous avez décidé?	You've decided?
pour moi	for me
steak-frites	steak and chips
filet de sole	fillet of sole
Je n'aime pas	I don't like
le poisson	fish
Je ne prends pas	I won't have
de dessert	any dessert
Comment voulez-vous	How do you want
votre steak?	your steak?
bien cuit	well done
comme boisson?	to drink?
une carafe	a carafe
de (vin) rouge	of red (wine)
un demi-litre	a half litre
d'eau minérale	of mineral water
vous voulez	you want
Bon appétit!	Enjoy your meal!

Dialogue

Waitress	Messieurs-dames, bonjour. Vous avez décidé?
Valérie	Pour moi, le filet de sole.
Jean-Marc	Un steak-frites, s'il vous plaît. Je n'aime pas le poisson.
Waitress	Comment voulez-vous votre steak, monsieur?
Jean-Marc	Bien cuit.
Waitress	Et comme boisson?
Valérie	Une carafe de rouge, s'il vous plaît.
Jean-Marc	Et un demi-litre d'eau minérale ...
Waitress	... Messieurs-dames! Filet de sole pour madame ... et votre steak, monsieur. Vous voulez un dessert? Glace? Tarte aux pommes?
Valérie	Non, je ne prends pas de dessert.
Waitress	Monsieur?
Jean-Marc	Non, merci.
Waitress	Alors bon appétit, messieurs-dames.

Exercices

1 Ecoutez!

Listen to the recording and tick the boxes according to each person's order.
(*Answers on page 126.*)

Customer	Steak	Fish	Wine	Water	Dessert
Man					
Woman					

2 Lisez! Ecrivez!
Rearrange these jumbled orders. (*Answers on page 126.*)
a) de Une rouge carafe vin
b) sole Pour de moi filet un
c) Je le pas n'aime poisson

3 ... et parlez français!
Order yourself a steak and chips (well done) and red wine, using the prompts
on your recording. (*Answers on page 126.*)

En français

1. The dialogue to this unit contains the first example of a *past event*, i.e. something that *has happened*.

Vous avez décidé?	You've decided? Have you decided?

You will come across more of these in later units.

2. Note the question form **voulez-vous** in **Comment voulez-vous votre steak?** It
is optional. You can also say **Comment vous voulez votre steak?**

3. To say 'not', put **ne** and **pas** round the verb.

Je <u>ne</u> prends <u>pas</u> de dessert	I'm not having any dessert

Ne changes to **n'** before a vowel.

Je <u>n'</u>aime <u>pas</u> le poisson	I don't like fish

En France

Steak-frites is France's most popular lunch-time dish. If you do not order your
steak **bien cuit** it will come rare (although a Frenchman would call it **à point**,
'medium') or extremely rare (**saignant**, lit. 'bleeding').
   Wine, red **(rouge)** or white **(blanc)**, served in **une carafe** or **un pichet** (jug)
will often be local wine, considerably cheaper than anything ordered by the bottle
(la bouteille) from **la carte des vins** (the wine list).

Travel by car

At the petrol station

Faites le plein	Fill up
ordinaire ou super?	2-star or 4-star?
sans plomb	lead-free
Je peux payer	Can I pay
par carte de crédit?	by credit card?
Signez ici	Sign here
Servez-vous	Serve yourself
Payez	Pay
à la caisse	at the till
libre-service	self-service
monnaie	change
Au revoir	Goodbye

Dialogues

1. **Motorist** — Faites le plein, s'il vous plaît.
   Attendant — Ordinaire ou super?
   Motorist — Super, sans plomb.
   Attendant — Alors, ça fait deux cent trente et un cinquante, mademoiselle.
   Motorist — Je peux payer par carte de crédit?
   Attendant — Oui, oui. Merci. Signez ici, s'il vous plaît.

2. **Motorist** — Trente litres de super, s'il vous plaît.
   Attendant — Servez-vous, monsieur. C'est libre-service. Payez à la caisse.
   Cashier — Alors 130 francs, s'il vous plaît. Deux cents francs, merci ... et votre monnaie ... soixante-dix francs. Merci, au revoir monsieur.

Exercices

1 Ecoutez!

Listen to the conversation and tick the boxes **VRAI** (True) or **FAUX** (False). (*Answers on page 126.*)

	VRAI	FAUX
a) The motorist wants 4-star petrol.		
b) She wants to fill her tank.		
c) She asks to pay by credit card.		
d) She is told to pay at the till.		

2 Lisez! Ecrivez!

a) Refer to the **En français** section, note 1, opposite, then put these eight numbers in ascending order of value. (*Answers on page 126.*)

trente-deux	soixante
vingt-quatre	quarante et un
cent cinquante-six	trente-six
dix-huit	deux cent dix

b) **Mots Croisés** (Crossword)

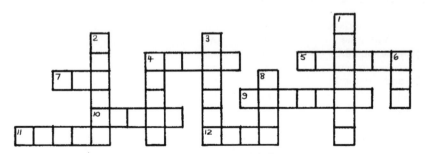

Horizontalement (*Clues across*)
4. Faites le ..... 5. Ça fait soixante ...... 7. Signez ... 9. Merci, et votre ....
10. ..... ou ordinaire? 11. ...... -service 12. .... plomb

Verticalement (*Clues down*)
1. La .... d'essence 2. Payez à la ...... 3. Trente ...... de super
4. Je peux ..... par carte de crédit? 6. .'.. vous plaît 8. Servez-....

3 ... et parlez français!
Take the motorist's part in the dialogue at the petrol station. (*Answers on page 126.*)

En français

1. Counting in hundreds is easy in French.

> **cent** 100   **deux cents** 200   **trois cents** 300 etc.

The final **s** is dropped before another number.

> **deux cent trente** 230   **trois cent cinquante-six** 356

2. *The imperative.* To give a command, use the imperative form of the verb, which is simply the **vous** form of the verb without the **vous**.

> **Vous signez** You sign   **Signez!** Sign!

En France

At the **station d'essence** (petrol station) the **pompiste** (pump attendant) may also offer to check your tyres (**pneus**), oil (**huile**) or water (**eau**). Avoid the pump labelled **gas-oil** or **gazole** unless you want diesel.

Talking about France

Paris

 Vocabulaire

les vacanciers	holidaymakers
une ville touristique	a tourist town
ma ville natale	my home town
je suis/vous êtes né	I was/you were born
dans le onzième	in the eleventh
arrondissement	(administrative) district of Paris
avant tout	above all
où	where
la capitale	the capital
un grand centre	a big centre
industriel	industrial
commercial	commercial
les étrangers pensent	foreigners think
que	that
un beau musée	a beautiful museum
en été	in summer
les Parisiens quittent	Parisians leave
leur ville	their town
pour aller	in order to go
Paris existe uniquement	Paris exists only
les Japonais	the Japanese

 Dialogue

Didier Pour les vacanciers, Paris est une ville touristique – la Cathédrale de Notre-Dame, la Tour Eiffel, la Seine, etc. Mais pour moi, c'est ma ville natale.

Claire Ah, vous êtes né à Paris?

Didier Oui, je suis né dans le onzième arrondissement.

Claire Pour moi, Paris c'est la ville où je travaille. C'est, avant tout, la capitale de la France et un grand centre industriel et commercial.

Didier Les étrangers pensent que Paris, c'est un beau musée, un grand spectacle pour les touristes.

Claire Oui, en été les Parisiens quittent leur ville pour aller en vacances et Paris existe uniquement pour les Américains et les Japonais!

Exercices

1 Ecoutez!

Listen again to the dialogue and then match the following pairs of phrases. For example, the first match is a–ii. Check your answers in the text and practise saying each one aloud. (*Answers on page 126.*)

a) En été les Parisiens
b) Pour moi, Paris est la ville
c) Pour les vacanciers,
d) Les étrangers pensent
e) Je suis né

i) dans le onzième arrondissement.
ii) quittent leur ville.
iii) où je travaille.
iv) que c'est un beau musée.
v) Paris est une ville touristique.

2 Ecrivez!

Use these pictures to complete the phrases about Paris. (*Answers on pages 126–7.*)

a)

Pour les vacanciers, _____

_____

b)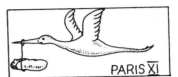

Oui, je suis né _____

c)

Pour moi, _____

_____

d)

Les Parisiens _____

En français

1. You have already met a number of **-ER** verbs used in the *present tense* and have seen how the ending changes according to whether it is 'I', 'you', 'he', 'she' or 'we' speak, work, live etc.

| **Je parl<u>e</u>** **il/elle arriv<u>e</u>** **nous habit<u>ons</u>** **vous parl<u>ez</u>** |

When the subject is 'they', the verb ends in **-ent**.

| **Les étrangers pens<u>ent</u> …** Foreigners think … |

But notice as you listen to the dialogue that the **-ent** is silent like the **e** in **Je parl<u>e</u>** and **Il arriv<u>e</u>**.

2. Most *adjectives* are placed *after* the noun they describe.

| **une ville <u>touristique</u>** a tourist town |

There are a few very common exceptions, e.g. **beau**, **grand**, **prochain**.

| **un <u>grand</u> centre touristique** a big tourist centre |

En France

Paris is divided into 20 administrative districts called **arrondissements**. Outside the capital the word **quartier** is generally used for a district of a town or city. Note **le Quartier Latin** – the Latin Quarter of Paris. The River Seine also divides the city into the **Rive Droite** (Right Bank) and **Rive Gauche** (Left Bank).

Language extra

These exercises provide extra practice in some of the more important language skills you have learnt in Units 1 to 12. Check your answers on page 127.

A. Verbs in the present tense

Remember: the dictionary gives verbs in their *infinitive* form. It is up to you to provide the right ending after **je** (I), **il** (he/it), **elle** (she/it), **nous** (we), **vous** (you), or **ils** (they). If you look up 'speak' in the dictionary you will find **parler**. To say 'We speak' you must remember to change the **-ER** to **-ONS**: **Nous parlons**.

In the exercise below change the infinitive form as required. Check with the verb tables on pages 131–2. (*Answers on page 127.*)

e.g. (PARLER) Nous _____   *Answer* Nous par<u>lons</u>

1.	(HABITER)	Nous _____	6.	(TRAVAILLER)	Je _____
2.	(PARLER)	Je _____	7.	(PARLER)	Elle _____
3.	(ARRIVER)	Il _____	8.	(HABITER)	J' _____
4.	(DESIRER)	Vous _____	9.	(TOURNER)	Vous _____
5.	(PENSER)	Ils _____	10.	(TRAVAILLER)	Nous _____

Some verbs do not follow the normal pattern and have to be learnt by heart. You will find these *irregular verbs* listed on pages 131–2. (*Answers on page 127.*)

e.g. (ETRE) Je _____   *Answer* Je suis

1.	(VENIR)	Je _____	6.	(PRENDRE)	Je _____
2.	(AVOIR)	Vous _____	7.	(POUVOIR)	Je _____
3.	(ETRE)	Vous _____	8.	(ALLER)	Je _____
4.	(ETRE)	Nous _____	9.	(VENIR)	Vous _____
5.	(ETRE)	Elle _____	10.	(FAIRE)	Ça _____

B. The imperative – telling someone to do something

Remember: To give a command simply use the **vous** form of the present tense – without the **vous**.
e.g. **Vous prenez** You take   **Prenez!** Take!
How would you tell someone:

1.	To give you a coffee	_____	– moi un café!
2.	To fill your tank up	_____	le plein!
3.	To turn left	_____	à gauche!
4.	To go straight on	_____	tout droit!
5.	To take the programme	_____	le programme!
6.	To sign here	_____	ici!

C. Negatives – how to say 'not'

Remember: **ne** before the verb and **pas** after the verb.
e.g. **Je <u>ne</u> suis <u>pas</u> français(e)   Je n'habite <u>pas</u> ici**
How would you say to a French person that you:

1.	don't speak well	**Je** _____
2.	don't like London	**Je** _____
3.	are not American	**Je** _____
4.	don't work here	**Je** _____
5.	are not on holiday	**Je** _____

Testez-vous!

Test yourself to see how much you can remember from Units 1 to 12. Check your answers on the recording.

In French, how do you ...

1. Greet a lady in the evening.
2. Ask 'Are you on holiday?'
3. Say 'I am English.'
4. Order two white coffees.
5. Ask 'What is the time?'
6. Ask 'How much is it?'
7. Say 'I work in London.'
8. Say 'I live in London.'
9. Say 'I come from London.'
10. Ask 'Is there is a bank nearby?'
11. Say 'I am on foot/in a car.'
12. Ask 'What number?'
13. Ask 'What time does the next train leave?'
14. Ask for a single/return ticket.
15. Ask for a kilo of tomatoes.
16. Ask for 100 grammes of olives.
17. Ask for a town plan.
18. Ask 'Is there something for the children?'
19. Order a steak and chips.
20. Ask for a full tank of petrol.
21. Ask 'Can I pay by credit card?'
22. Ask the way to Nantes.
23. Say 'I was born in ...'
24. Say 'It's my home town.'
25. Say goodbye.

In the café

Ordering drinks and snacks

Vocabulaire

un café au lait	a white coffee
un thé au citron	a lemon tea
Je peux avoir du sucre?	Can I have some sugar?
quelque chose à manger	something to eat
des sandwichs	(some) sandwiches
des galettes	(some) savoury pancakes
des pizzas	(some) pizzas
fromage	cheese
jambon	ham
salami	salami
je préfère	I prefer
un sandwich au fromage	a cheese sandwich
une tarte aux pommes	an apple tart
des tartes aux fraises	(some) strawberry tarts
nous avons seulement	we have only
aujourd'hui	today

Dialogue

Waitress	Messieurs-dames. Qu'est-ce que vous voulez?
First customer	Un café au lait, s'il vous plaît.
Second customer	Pour moi, un thé au citron.
Waitress	Voilà, un café au lait, un thé au citron.
First customer	Merci. Je peux avoir du sucre, s'il vous plaît?
Waitress	Oui, tout de suite, madame.
Second customer	Vous avez quelque chose à manger?
Waitress	Des sandwichs, des galettes, des pizzas.
Second customer	Qu'est-ce que vous avez comme sandwichs?
Waitress	Fromage, jambon, salami.
Second customer	Je préfère le fromage.
Waitress	Un sandwich au fromage. Et pour madame?
First customer	Je voudrais une tarte aux pommes.
Waitress	Nous avons seulement des tartes aux fraises aujourd'hui.
First customer	Alors une tarte aux fraises.
Waitress	Ça fait 52F50, s'il vous plaît, monsieur.

Exercices

1 Ecoutez!

Listen to the orders and tick the boxes where you hear the item actually ordered. (*Answers on page 127.*)

White coffee		Ham sandwich		White wine	
Black coffee		Apple tart		Lemon tea	

2 Lisez! Ecoutez!
Tick the correct price for each of the six items on your recording.
(*Answers on page 127.*)

a) 32F50 ___	23F50 ___	d) 15F00 ___	50F00 ___
b) 42F60 ___	53F70 ___	e) 59F60 ___	49F50 ___
c) 16F50 ___	6F50 ___	f) 24F00 ___	43F00 ___

3 ... et parlez français!
Order something to eat and drink for yourself and a friend. The waiter will start
with **Messieurs-dames?** Use the prompts below to complete the conversation.
(*Answers on page 127.*)

1. Order one beer and one lemon tea.
2. Ask 'Do you have anything to eat?'
3. Say 'What kind of sandwiches have you got?'
4. Say 'I prefer the cheese' and 'I would like a strawberry tart'.

En français

1. See how **au** (masc.), **à la** (fem.) and **aux** (plural) are used to say something is
made 'with' ham, milk, etc.

un sandwich <u>au</u> jambon	a ham sandwich
une tarte <u>à la</u> crème	a cream tart

Similarly, **du** (masc.), **de la** (fem.) and **des** (plural) are used to say 'some':

> **Je peux avoir <u>du</u> sucre?**
> **<u>des</u> sandwichs, <u>des</u> galettes, <u>des</u> pizzas.**

In the examples above and in the dialogue, note the forms **au**, **aux** and **du**, **des**,
which replace '**à le**', '**à les**', '**de le**' and '**de les**'.

2. *Accents*. Just occasionally an accent on the letter **a** can change the *meaning*,
as with **a** meaning 'has' and **à** meaning 'at' or 'to'. Listen out too for the slight
difference in *pronunciation* between **é** and **è**, e.g. in the word **préfère** in the
dialogue to this unit. Finally, note that capitals are usually written without accents.

En France

More about ...
Tea and coffee – If you prefer your coffee white, ask for **un café au lait**, **un café
crème**, or just **un crème** (Unit 2). A black coffee is **un express**, **un café noir**, **un
café nature** or simply **un café**. There is little enthusiasm in France for tea, except
perhaps for the iced variety – **thé glacé** – in the summer. Otherwise tea is drunk
weak and usually **au citron** rather than **au lait**.
Sandwiches – The French may have borrowed the word but there the resem-
blance ends. In France **un sandwich** is a crispy **baguette** (French stick) with a
generous, deliciously fresh filling – with a glass of wine, a meal in itself!

UNIT 15 At the hotel

Checking in

Vocabulaire

à deux lits	with twin beds
avec grand lit	with double bed
salle de bains privée	private bathroom
un peu cher	a bit expensive
une chambre moins chère	a less expensive room
juste	just
les WC et le lavabo	the toilet and washbasin
une seule nuit	only one night
je la prends	I'll take it
remplir cette fiche	to fill out this form
petit déjeuner	breakfast
compris	included
en supplément	extra
par personne	per person
vous pouvez la laisser	you can leave it
devant l'hôtel	in front of the hotel
au premier étage	on (lit. at) the first floor

Dialogue

Tourist	Vous avez une chambre pour la nuit?
Receptionist	Pour deux personnes? Oui, une chambre à deux lits, avec salle de bains privée, c'est 450 francs.
Tourist	C'est un peu cher.
Receptionist	J'ai une chambre moins chère avec grand lit, à 260 francs, mais sans salle de bains. Il y a juste les WC et le lavabo.
Tourist	Oui, ça va. C'est juste pour une nuit. Je la prends.
Receptionist	Très bien, monsieur. Voulez-vous remplir cette fiche, s'il vous plaît?
Tourist	Oui. Euh, le petit déjeuner est compris?
Receptionist	Non, c'est en supplément. C'est 35 francs par personne.
Tourist	Est-ce qu'il y a un parking pour la voiture?
Receptionist	Vous pouvez la laisser devant l'hôtel, monsieur. Voici votre clé. Numéro 12, au premier étage.

Exercices

1 **Ecoutez!**

Listen to the hotel receptionist giving details about your room and tick the correct answers to the following questions: (*Answers on page 127.*)

a) Is the price of the room .... 230F? ☐ 350F? ☐

b) Does the room have ....WC only? ☐ bathroom? ☐

c) Is the room on the .... 2nd floor? ☐ 3rd floor? ☐

d) Is breakfast .... included? ☐ 25F each? ☐ 30F each? ☐

e) Should the car be parked .... in front? ☐ behind? ☐

2 Lisez!

Match the halves of these sentences. (*Answers on page 127*.)

a)	Vous avez une chambre	i)	cette fiche?
b)	Est-ce qu'il y a un parking	ii)	pour la nuit?
c)	Vous pouvez la laisser	iii)	est compris?
d)	J'ai une chambre avec	iv)	pour la voiture?
e)	Voulez-vous remplir	v)	devant l'hôtel.
f)	Le petit déjeuner	vi)	grand lit.

3 ... et parlez français!

Now re-create the dialogue at the hotel reception desk using the prompts below. (*Answers on page 127*.)

1. I would like a room for two people please.
2. That's a bit expensive.
3. Yes, that's all right. Ask 'Is breakfast included?'
4. Is there a car park?

En français

1. In French the *object pronoun* for 'it' comes before the verb.

I'll *take it*	**Je la prends**
You can *leave it*	**Vous pouvez la laisser**

In the first of these examples in the dialogue 'it' refers to the room – **la chambre**, while in the second 'it' stands for the car – **la voiture**. These are both feminine words. If they were masculine words we would say **Je le prends, Vous pouvez le laisser**.

The plural of both **le** and **la** is **les** 'them'.

I'll take them	**Je les prends**

2. Still on the subject of gender, you have now met two words for 'this' – **ce** for masculine nouns, **cette** for feminine nouns.

Ce soir	This evening (Unit 9)
Cette fiche	This form (Unit 15)

The plural of both **ce** and **cette** is **ces**:

Ces soirs	These evenings	**Ces fiches**	These forms

En France

Whatever accommodation you decide on, you can check the details on the back of the door in your room where management (**la direction**) is required by law to display prices – the basic price of the room (**prix de la chambre**), and the price for **le petit déjeuner**, as well as rates for **demi-pension** (half-board) and **pension complète** (full board) if available. If you are unlucky enough to see the sign **Complet** outside the hotel, however, there will be no room at all – **Hôtel Complet** means 'Hotel Full'.

Numbers

Booking a room

Vocabulaire

désolé	sorry	soixante-dix	70
Essayez	Try	soixante et onze	71
Attendez	Wait	soixante-douze	72
je vous donne	I'll give you	quatre-vingts	80
le numéro de téléphone	the phone number	quatre-vingt-un	81
je vous remercie	(I) thank you	quatre-vingt-deux	82
Allô!	Hello! (on the phone)	quatre-vingt-dix	90
parfait	perfect, fine	quatre-vingt-onze	91
réserver	to reserve	quatre-vingt-dix-neuf	99
par téléphone	by phone	cent	100
valable	valid		
décembre	December		
je répète	I repeat		
réservé	reserved		

Dialogues

First receptionist	Je suis désolée, monsieur, l'hôtel est complet. Essayez l'Hôtel Mercure – 78 rue du Moulin. Attendez, je vous donne le numéro de téléphone.
Tourist	Oui?
First receptionist	Alors, c'est le 94.72.80.34.
Tourist	Je vous remercie, madame. Au revoir.
Second receptionist	Allô! Hôtel Mercure.
Tourist	Bonsoir. Est-ce que vous avez une chambre pour deux personnes pour ce soir?
Second receptionist	Oui monsieur. J'ai une chambre avec salle de bains à 475F, monsieur.
Tourist	C'est parfait. Je peux réserver par téléphone?
Second receptionist	Vous avez une carte de crédit, monsieur?
Tourist	Oui, c'est le 74 80 92 98 30 12. La carte est valable jusqu'à décembre 99.
Second receptionist	Merci, monsieur. Je répète: le 74 80 92 98 30 12. Votre chambre est réservée jusqu'à 7 heures.
Tourist	Merci beaucoup, madame. Au revoir.

Hôtel ** GRANVELLE

13, RUE LECOURBE
25000 BESANÇON
TÉLÉPHONE 81 81 33 92
TÉLÉCOPIE 81 81 31 77

Un hôtel de caractère au pied de la citadelle,
au centre de la vieille ville,
dans une cour intérieure avec parking privé.

A deux pas de l'Opéra Théâtre

Exercices

1 Ecoutez!
Listen to the recording and write down the ten numbers. (*Answers on page 127.*)

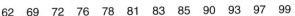

2 Lisez!
(Read the **En français, En France** section before doing this exercise.) The following telephone numbers have been jotted down in a hurry and one digit is wrong in each number. The correct version is on the recording. Listen and write in the corrections on the line beneath. (*Answers on page 127.*)

01- 21 - 03 - 89
61- 93 - 27 - 86
71 - 17 - 80 - 99
52- 11 - 34 - 66

3 ... et parlez français!
a) Read aloud the following numbers and repeat them after you hear them on your recording.

  62   69   72   76   78   81   83   85   90   93   97   99

b) Read the numbers again, adding 1 to each, i.e. 63, 70, etc.

Check the correct answers on your recording.

En français, En France

1.   There are no new numbers to learn for 70, 80 and 90. Instead, the French make them up with combinations of **soixante** and **vingt**.

70	**soixante-dix**	'60–10'
71	**soixante et onze**	'60 and 11'
72	**soixante-douze**	'60–12'
80	**quatre-vingts**	'4–20s'
81	**quatre-vingt-un**	'4–20s–1'
82	**quatre-vingt-deux**	'4–20s–2'
90	**quatre-vingt-dix**	'4–20s–10'
99	**quatre-vingt-dix-neuf**	'4–20s–19'

2.   French telephone numbers begin with **le** when spoken. Whether written or spoken, telephone numbers are given in twos, so that 24.13.52.75 is **vingt-quatre – treize – cinquante-deux – soixante-quinze**. If the first digit of a pair is 0, say **zéro**. So 40 is **quarante**, while 04 is **zéro quatre**.

3.   Be aware of the characteristic French way of handwriting the numbers *1, 4, 7* and *9* – it will save many a wrong phone number and prevent misunderstandings when reading restaurant and hotel bills!

Talking about yourself

Family and work

Vocabulaire

mon mari s'appelle	my husband is called
comme secrétaire	as secretary
une compagnie/une entreprise	a company
qui importe	which imports
qui fabrique	which manufactures
ordinateurs	computers
pièces	parts
l'industrie automobile	the motor industry
pharmacien	chemist
ingénieur	engineer
journaliste	journalist
étudiant(e)	student
professeur	teacher
marié	married
célibataire	unmarried, single
je voyage beaucoup	I travel a lot
en France	in France
à l'étranger	abroad
à son compte	for himself
notre fils/fille	our son/daughter
depuis 5 ans	for 5 years

Dialogues

Je m'appelle Pascale Martin. Depuis 3 ans je travaille comme secrétaire dans une compagnie qui importe des ordinateurs. J'ai 36 ans et je suis mariée. J'ai deux enfants. Mon mari s'appelle Jean-Luc. Il est pharmacien dans une entreprise américaine.

Je m'appelle Georges Renan. J'ai 25 ans. Je suis célibataire. Je travaille comme ingénieur dans une entreprise qui fabrique des pièces pour l'industrie automobile et je voyage beaucoup en France et à l'étranger.

Je m'appelle Nathalie Moreau. Je suis journaliste. Mon mari travaille à son compte. Notre fils Raymond a 30 ans, il est professeur. Notre fille Chantal est étudiante, elle habite à Paris depuis 5 ans.

Exercices

1 Ecoutez!

Listen to four people speaking about themselves and write in the missing information in the boxes on the next page. Remember a French speaker may also be Belgian – **belge** – or Swiss – **suisse**. (*Answers on page 127.*)

Name	Nationality	Family Status	Occupation	Age	Children
Céline Blanc	Belgian				—
Jules Forget					Son 3yrs
Laure Simon		single			
Jean Camus			teacher		

2 Ecoutez! Lisez! Ecrivez!
Listen again to Jean Camus in Exercise 1. Using the **En France** section below fill in his personal **fiche voyageur** (registration form). (*Answers on page 127.*)

Nom .... Nationalité ....
Prénom .... Domicile habituel ....
Occupation .... Situation de famille ....

Note: **domicile habituel** – permanent place of residence; **situation de famille** – family status.

3 ... et parlez français!
Imagine you are Pascale Martin's husband Jean-Luc, from the first section of dialogue on the facing page and talk about yourself and your wife. Check on your recording to see what Jean-Luc might have said.

En français

1. To state your age in French, say 'I have' – **J'ai**, plus the number of years.

J'ai 25 ans	I have 25 years, i.e. I am 25
Ma fille a 10 ans	My daughter has 10 years, i.e. she is 10

2. To say that you have been doing something (and still are), just say 'I live', 'I work' with the word **depuis** – 'for/since'.

Nous habitons à Paris depuis deux ans	We have been living in Paris *for* two years
Je travaille à Londres depuis février	I have been working in London *since* February

En France

You may be asked to fill in a **fiche** (form) when you check into your hotel. Apart from stating your **nationalité** and your **occupation** on forms you will also need to know that your **nom** is your surname and your **prénom** is your first name. If you are single, write **célibataire** in the **situation de famille** space. If you are a woman remember to add an extra **-e** to **marié**, **séparé** or **divorcé**.

UNIT 8 Out and about

Asking for directions

Vocabulaire

pour aller	how do I get (to)
hein?	eh?
compliqué	complicated
mais attention	but be careful
il ferme	it closes
Prenez le bus (autobus)	Take the bus
fréquent	frequent
toutes les 5 minutes	every 5 minutes
il faut acheter	you must buy
vos billets	your tickets
d'abord	first (of all)
au café-tabac	at the café-tabac
Euh	Er, uhm
arrêt d'autobus	bus stop
derrière	behind
descendre	(to) get off
Place du Marché	Market Square
vous verrez	you will see
en face	opposite

Dialogue

Tourist	Pardon, monsieur. Pour aller au Syndicat d'Initiative, s'il vous plaît?
Passer-by	C'est assez loin d'ici, hein? C'est un peu compliqué. Vous êtes en voiture?
Tourist	Non, nous sommes à pied.
Passer-by	A pied? Mais attention, il ferme à une heure. Prenez le bus, mademoiselle.
Tourist	Ils sont fréquents, les autobus?
Passer-by	Toutes les cinq minutes. Il faut acheter vos billets d'abord au café-tabac.
Tourist	Euh, où est le café?
Passer-by	Le café? C'est là-bas. Vous avez l'arrêt d'autobus derrière le café. Puis il faut descendre à la Place du Marché et vous verrez le Syndicat d'Initiative en face.
Tourist	Merci beaucoup, monsieur.

Exercices

1 **Ecoutez!**

A tourist is being given directions to get to the bank before it closes. Listen and fill in the missing details. (*Answers on page 127.*)

Take bus no. ____. Buses run every _____. Tickets from café which is _____. Fare is ____ francs. Bus stop is _____. Get off at _____. Bank is _____. Bank closes at ____ o'clock.

2 Lisez!

Match the halves of these sentences. (*Answers on page 127.*)

a) Il faut	i) à pied.
b) Nous sommes	ii) le Syndicat d'Initiative.
c) Il ferme	iii) fréquents?
d) Vous verrez	iv) descendre à la Place du Marché.
e) Ils sont	v) à une heure.

3 ... et parlez français!

You stop a passer-by to find out the way to the **Hôtel Mercure**. Use the prompts below to ask the questions. You start by attracting the attention of a woman passer-by. (*Answers on page 127.*)

1. Excuse me, Miss.
2. How do we get to the **Hôtel Mercure**, please?
3. No, we're on foot.
4. Are the buses frequent?
5. Where is the café?

En français

1. In this unit you have met **nous sommes** – 'we are' and **ils sont** – 'they are', from the verb **être** – 'to be'. Make a special effort to learn by heart all the forms of **être** that you have met so far.

je suis	I am
il/elle est	he/she is
nous sommes	we are
vous êtes	you are
ils/elles sont	they are

Note: **elles** is used only if 'they' are *all feminine*. If masculine, or mixed gender, use **ils**.

2. **Il faut** – literally, 'it is necessary', is a very important way of saying what has to be done.

Il faut acheter vos billets	You must buy your tickets

3. **Vos** is the plural of **votre** – 'your'.

<u>votre</u> **steak**	your steak	<u>vos</u> **billets**	your ticket<u>s</u>

Also note **notre/nos** (our). You will find the complete table of these possessive adjectives in Unit 40.

En France

It is as well to be aware of closing times in shops and offices in France. Shops as a rule open early and close late, but often close for two hours at lunch, while many banks and basic food shops – bakers excepted – are closed Mondays for all or part of the day.

Public transport

Reserving a seat on the TGV

Vocabulaire

demain matin	tomorrow morning
Il faut changer	You have to change
réserver des places	(to) reserve seats
un rapide	a fast train
le TGV	the TGV (high-speed) intercity train
une correspondance	a connection
un tarif réduit	a reduced fare
deux adultes	two adults
C'est mieux	That's better
aussi	also
ici	here
Quel âge ont-ils?	How old are they?

Dialogue

Traveller	Est-ce qu'il y a un train direct pour St-Etienne demain matin?
Employee	Non, monsieur. Il faut changer à Lyon. Il y a un rapide à 9h12.
Traveller	Il arrive à quelle heure à Lyon?
Employee	A 11h45, monsieur. Il y a aussi le TGV qui part à 9h10. Il arrive à 10h38. Puis vous avez une correspondance à 11h10 pour St-Etienne.
Traveller	C'est mieux. Je peux réserver des places ici?
Employee	Combien de personnes?
Traveller	Quatre personnes. Deux adultes et deux enfants. Il y a un tarif réduit pour les enfants?
Employee	Quel âge ont-ils?
Traveller	11 ans et 14 ans.
Employee	Alors deux adultes, deux demi-tarifs. 840F, s'il vous plaît.

Exercices

1 Ecoutez!

Numbers practice. Listen to the recording and write down, in figures, the following details. (*Answers on page 127.*)

a) Departure time _____

b) Time of arrival in Lyon _____

c) Time of connection _____

d) Time of arrival in Grenoble _____

e) Age of children _____

f) Price of children's tickets _____

g) Total price _____

2 Lisez! Ecrivez!

Try this **mots croisés** (crossword). You will find all the words you need in the dialogue and in the **En France** section opposite. (*Answers on page 127.*)

Horizontalement   3 Train à grande vitesse.   6. Vous avez une ____ à 11h10.
7. Deux ____ -tarifs.   8. Trans-Europ-Express.

Verticalement   1 Il faut réserver votre ____.   2 Il faut ____ à Lyon.
3 Deux demi- ____.   4 Il y a un ____ à 9h12.   5 Tarif ____ pour les enfants.

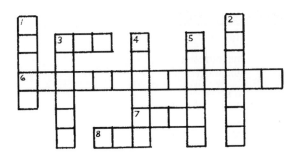

3 ... et parlez français!

Re-create the scene at the booking office from the facing page. Use the prompts below to complete the conversation on the recording. (*Answers on page 127.*) You start by asking: 'Can I reserve seats here?'

1. Say 'St-Etienne'.
2. Say 'Two adults and three children'. Then ask 'Is there a reduction for the children?'
3. Say '6, 8 and 11 years'.

En français

Pronunciation – Listen carefully and try your best to copy French *nasal sounds* which are such a characteristic feature of the language. The following phrases from the vocabulary and dialogue of the present unit are on your recording after Exercise 3.

> i)   **dem<u>ain</u> mat<u>in</u>**
> ii) **il faut cha<u>nger</u>**
> iii) **<u>un</u> rapide**
> iv) **Quel âge <u>ont</u>-ils?**

Always try to make the nasal sound *without pronouncing the 'n'.*

En France

The **TGV – train à grande vitesse** (high speed train) – now travels to most cities in France. Thanks to the **TGV**, travellers can now make the journey from London Waterloo to **Paris Gare du Nord** in just 3 hours. Other types of train are the **TEE** (luxury **Trans-Europe-Express**), the **rapide**, the **express** (long-distance but slower than the **rapide**), and the **train omnibus** – local train which stops at all stations.

 Shopping

At the jeweller's

 ### Vocabulaire

voir	(to) see
ce bracelet	this bracelet
cette montre	this watch
en argent	in silver
joli	pretty
exquis	exquisite
Lequel?	Which one?
Celui-ci/là? **Celle-ci/là?**	This/that one?
n'est-ce pas?	isn't it?
certainement	certainly
Quel dommage!	What a pity!
Il coûte combien?	How much does it cost?
C'est quel prix?	What price is it?
mille	thousand
Elle me plaît	I like it (lit. It pleases me)
Je vais la prendre	I'll take it
C'est pour offrir?	Is it for a gift?

Dialogue

Customer	Est-ce que je peux voir ce bracelet, s'il vous plaît?
Assistant	Certainement, monsieur. Lequel? Celui-ci?
Customer	Non, celui-là.
Assistant	Voilà. Il est très joli, n'est-ce pas?
Customer	Oui, il est très beau. Il coûte combien?
Assistant	Celui-ci est en argent, monsieur. Il coûte 2150 francs.
Customer	Ah non, c'est beaucoup trop cher. Quel dommage! Attendez, je peux voir cette montre?
Assistant	Celle-ci?
Customer	Oui. Elle est exquise! C'est quel prix?
Assistant	1200 francs, monsieur.
Customer	Elle me plaît beaucoup. Oui, je vais la prendre.
Assistant	Très bien, monsieur. C'est pour offrir?

Exercices

 1 Ecoutez!

Listen to another conversation between a customer and the jeweller's assistant and answer these questions. (*Answers on page 127.*)

a) What does the customer ask to see?
b) Where was it made?
c) Why does he not buy it?
d) What is he shown next?
e) How much does it cost?

2 Lisez!
Fill in the gaps with the following. (*Answers on page 127.*)

celui   ce   celle   c'est   cette

a) Je peux voir _____ montre?
b) _____ beaucoup trop cher.
c) Lequel? _____ -ci?
d) _____ -ci? Oui, elle est exquise.
e) Je peux voir _____ bracelet?

3 ... et parlez français!
You go to the jeweller's to buy a watch and end up buying a bracelet! Use the prompts below and remember – **montre** is feminine and **bracelet** is masculine. Check the **En français** section below. (*Answers on page 127.*)

1. Ask 'Can I see this watch, please?'
2. Say 'No, that one.'
3. Say it's very pretty, and ask how much it costs.
4. Say 'What a pity, it's too dear.' Then point and say 'Can I see this bracelet?'
5. Ask 'What price is it?'
6. Say 'I like it a lot. Yes, I'll take it.'

En français

1. Note different forms.

		Masculine	Feminine
1.	This	**Ce** bracelet	**Cette** montre
	This one	**Celui**-ci	**Celle**-ci
	That one	**Celui**-là	**Celle**-là
2.	Which?	**Quel** bracelet?	**Quelle** montre?
	Which one?	**Lequel?**	**Laquelle?**

Notes: i) The plural of both **ce** and **cette** is **ces**.
        ii) For the plural forms of **celle/quel/quelle** – just add **s**.
             The plural of **celui** is **ceux**.
             The plurals of **lequel, laquelle** are **lesquels, lesquelles**.
        iii) **Quel/Quelle** is also used in exclamations: **Quel dommage!**

2. You will often hear the expressions **hein?** (Unit 18) and the more formal **n'est-ce pas?** (from this unit). These are tagged on to the end of a phrase to mean something like 'isn't it?', 'aren't they?', 'don't you think?', 'you know?' **Vous êtes français, n'est-ce pas?** – 'You're French, aren't you?'; **C'est un peu cher, hein?** – 'It's a bit expensive, isn't it?'

3. The word for 'thousand' – **mille** – does not add **s** in the plural: 1000F – 'mille francs'; 2000F – 'deux mille francs'.

En France

When you buy **un souvenir** or **un cadeau** (present) you will often be asked **C'est pour offrir?** – Is it to offer? i.e. Do you want it gift-wrapped? This extra service is normally included in the price in French shops.

Services

At the post office

UNIT 21

 Vocabulaire

envoyer	to send
ce paquet	this parcel
timbres	stamps
six cartes postales	six postcards
la bonne queue	the right queue
au guichet	to the counter
un billet de 500 francs	a 500 franc note
votre monnaie	your change
vous pouvez changer	you can change
en Espagne	to Spain
l'Angleterre	England
le Portugal	Portugal
l'Allemagne	Germany
l'Italie	Italy
les Etats-Unis	the United States
l'Amérique	America
les pays	the countries
l'Union Européenne	the European Union
Voyons	Let's see
Oh là là!	Wow! Oh dear!

Dialogue

Customer Je voudrais envoyer ce paquet en Espagne. Je suis dans la bonne queue?

Clerk Non, il faut aller au guichet numéro 3.

Customer Et pour les timbres, c'est ici? Bon, alors j'ai six cartes postales – deux pour l'Angleterre, deux pour le Portugal, une pour l'Allemagne et une pour les Etats-Unis. Puis j'ai une lettre pour l'Italie.

Clerk Voyons, pour les cartes postales c'est 3F20 pour les pays de l'Union Européenne, 4F10 pour l'Amérique et 4F40 pour la lettre. Ça fait 24F50, s'il vous plaît, mademoiselle.

Customer Euh, est-ce que vous pouvez changer un billet de 500 francs?

Clerk Oh là là! Attendez, 500 francs. 24F50 ... et votre monnaie, voilà mademoiselle.

Exercices

1 Ecoutez!

What are these customers asking for? Write the missing information in the boxes below. (*Answers on page 127.*)

Customer	Destinations	No. of postcards	No. of parcels	No. of letters	Total price
1					
2					
3					

2 Ecrivez!

To complete this crossword you will need the names of four countries (from this unit) and two cities (from Unit 1). Look back if you are stuck! (*Answers on page 127.*)

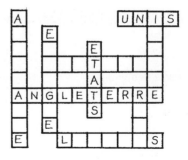

3 ... et parlez français!

Using the recording from Exercise 1, stop the tape as necessary and speak the parts of customers 1, 2 and 3. Use the correct answers from the grid in Exercise 1 as prompts. Check your answers on the recording.

En français

Most European countries end in **e** and are feminine – **la France**, **l'** before a vowel: **l'Espagne**, **l'Angleterre**, etc. **Le Portugal** is one of the few masculine countries.

To say 'to' or 'in' a country, put **en** before feminine and **au** before masculine countries.

en France, en Angleterre, en Amérique	(fem.)
au Portugal, au Canada, au Japon	(masc.)

For 'in/to the United State<u>s</u>' use the plural form **aux**.

aux Etats-Unis

'South America', incidentally, is **l'Amérique du Sud**.

En France

You can buy stamps from a **café-tabac** as well as at the post office – **le bureau de poste**, usually called simply **la poste** – generally open from 8 a.m. till 7 p.m. weekdays. You will recognise the post office by the sign **PTT** (**Postes-Télégraphes-Téléphones**) or **P et T** (**Postes et Télécommunications**) outside. Inside look for signs over each **guichet** such as **Affranchissements** (Postage) or **Timbres** (Stamps), **Mandats-Poste** (Money Orders), and of course the **Poste Restante** service for travellers without a permanent address.

Eating out

Aperitifs and starters

Vocabulaire

une table	a table
Suivez-moi	Follow me
la carte	the menu
la carte des vins	the wine list
un apéritif	an aperitif
pastis	pastis (aniseed and water)
comme entrée?	as starter course?
Vous avez choisi?	Have you chosen?
nous allons prendre	we're going to have
j'hésite	I'm hesitating
je ne sais pas	I don't know
Qu'est-ce que vous proposez?	What do you suggest?
la demi-douzaine	the half-dozen
j'ai horreur des escargots	snails horrify me; I hate snails

MENU	
Entrées	
Soupe à l'oignon	Onion soup
Fruits de mer	Mixed shellfish
Crudités	Raw, chopped vegetables
Salade mixte	Mixed salad
Moules marinière	Mussels in white wine
Escargots (En supplément)	Snails (extra)

Dialogue

Customer 1 Vous avez une table pour deux personnes, s'il vous plaît?

Waitress Suivez-moi, messieurs-dames. Voici la carte. Et la carte des vins. Vous prenez un apéritif?

Customer 2 Un kir et un pastis, s'il vous plaît.

Waitress Et comme entrée? Soupe à l'oignon, fruits de mer, crudités, salade mixte, moules marinière, escargots?

Customer 1 J'hésite, hein … Euh, qu'est-ce que vous proposez?

Waitress Les moules sont excellentes.

Customer 1 Je ne sais pas. Les escargots sont en supplément?

Waitress 20 francs la demi-douzaine, monsieur.

Customer 2 Moi, j'ai horreur des escargots. Je vais prendre la salade.

Customer 1 Oui? Bon d'accord, moi aussi …

Waitress … Vous avez choisi, messieurs-dames?

Customer 2 Oui. Nous allons prendre la salade.

Exercices

1 **Ecoutez!**

Listen to three customers ordering aperitifs and starters and put a tick or a cross in the box to indicate whether the waiter has taken down the order correctly. (*Answers on page 127.*)

	Aperitif			*Starter course*	
Diner A	.... beer	☐	.... onion soup	☐
Diner B	.... pastis	☐	.... snails	☐
Diner C	.... kir	☐	.... mixed salad	☐

2 Ecrivez!
Refer to the vocabulary and the **En France** section and unscramble these
seven aperitifs and starter dishes. (*Answers on page 127.*)

a) USCREDIT ....

b) BENTUNDO ....

c) REDPON ....

d) GOATCRESS ....

e) DALASE TEXIM ....

f) PASSIT ....

g) SLUMEO REARMINIE ....

3 ... et parlez français!
Refer again to the **En France** section below, then order for yourself and three
friends using the prompts below. (*Answers on page 127.*)

1. Ask the waiter if he has a table for four people, please.
2. Order a Pastis, two kirs and an orange juice.
3. Now order mussels, snails, onion soup and mixed salad.

En français

1. You have already met **Excusez-moi** (Unit 6) and **Donnez-moi** (Unit 8). In this
unit **Suivez-moi** – 'Follow me' – appears in the dialogue. You will hear **moi** – 'me'
very frequently in conversation, especially after prepositions, e.g. **pour moi** – 'for
me', **avec moi** – 'with me'. Also in the expression **C'est moi** – 'It's me'.

2. Note the French for 'onion soup' – **soupe à l'oignon**. **Au** and **à la** both change
to **à l'** before a word beginning with a vowel.

café <u>au</u> lait	tarte <u>à</u> l'orange

Du and **de la** also change – to **de l'** – before a vowel.

du pain	some bread	**de l'argent**	some money

En France

For your **apéritif** you might order **un Dubonnet**, **un Pernod**, or a fruit juice, perhaps **un jus d'orange** (orange juice). For your **entrée** or **hors-d'œuvre**, look out
for soup appearing on your menu as **potage** or as a thick creamy **velouté**, while
a **bisque** is another rich soup made from **crevettes** (prawns) or **homard** (lob-
ster). Also featuring on the menu may be **pâté maison** (home-made pâté), **pâté
de foie gras** (rich liver pâté), or of course the famously French **escargots** or
cuisses de grenouilles (frogs' legs), almost certain to be **en supplément**.

Travel by car
Hiring a car

Vocabulaire

louer	to hire
la semaine prochaine	next week
à partir de	starting from
lundi prochain	next Monday
Eh bien	Well
quelque chose de plus petit	something smaller
Ça vous va?	Does that suit you?
Tout compris?	Everything included?
kilométrage illimité	unlimited mileage
assurance	insurance
TVA	VAT
c'est d'accord	fine, agreed
il me faut	I need
une pièce d'identité	some identity
votre permis de conduire	your driving licence
vous acceptez	you accept

Dialogue

Receptionist Monsieur?
Customer Je voudrais louer une voiture pour la semaine prochaine.
Receptionist Oui, monsieur. Pour combien de jours?
Customer Pour une semaine, à partir de lundi prochain. Qu'est-ce que vous avez comme voitures?
Receptionist Eh bien, nous avons une Peugeot 506 …
Customer Non, je préfère quelque chose de plus petit.
Receptionist Il y a une Renault 5. Ça vous va?
Customer C'est parfait. C'est combien pour la semaine?
Receptionist Alors, c'est 1970F.
Customer Tout compris?
Receptionist Oui, monsieur. Kilométrage illimité, assurance, TVA. Tout compris.
Customer Bon, c'est d'accord.
Receptionist Il me faut une pièce d'identité et votre permis de conduire, monsieur … Merci. Comment voulez-vous payer?
Customer Vous acceptez les cartes de crédit?
Receptionist Certainement, monsieur.

Exercices

1 **Ecoutez!**
Listen to three more customers as they arrange a car rental. Fill in the missing information below. (*Answers on page 127.*)

Customer	Type of car	For how long	Rate per day
A			
B			
C			

2 Lisez! Ecrivez!
Unscramble these sentences. (*Answers on page 127.*)
a) voudrais pour voiture jours Je une trois louer
b) plus quelque Je de préfère petit chose
c) prochain partir A de lundi
d) pièce Il et conduire d'identité me faut permis de votre une

3 … et parlez français!
Take part in a scene in the car rental office. The female assistant greets you
with '**Bonjour!**' Use the prompts below and refer to the **En français** section.
(*Answers on page 127.*)

1. Say you would like to rent a car for tomorrow.
2. Say 'A large one. We are four adults.'
3. Ask if she has something cheaper.
4. Ask if she accepts credit cards.

En français

Note the use of **quelque chose** with **de plus/moins** … followed by the masculine
adjective (**petit**, **cher**, etc.), to say 'something more/less …'.

quelque chose <u>de</u> plus petit	something smaller
quelque chose <u>de</u> moins cher	something less expensive

Plus is also used for the English 'plus'.

plus TVA	plus VAT

En France

A car rental agency is a **bureau de location**. Cars may also be rented from main
line (**SNCF**) railway stations. Types of vehicle might be **un break** or **une familiale**
– 'estate car', as opposed to **une berline** – 'saloon car', or **une (voiture)**
décapotable (convertible). In case you are not **au fait** (knowledgeable) with
makes of motor car – the French names to recognise are of course **Citroën**,
Peugeot and **Renault**. Look for rates which include **kilométrage illimité** – 'unlimited mileage'.

Talking about France

The regions of France

Vocabulaire

département	department (of France)
qui se trouve	which is situated (lit. 'finds itself')
vous connaissez	you know
je ne connais pas bien	I don't know well
pas toutes	not all
Il y en a 22	There are 22 of them
par exemple	for example
la Bretagne	Brittany
du Midi	of the Midi
Qu'est-ce que c'est?	What's that?
la moitié Sud	the Southern half
y compris	including
à mon avis	in my opinion
les plus belles	the most beautiful
les Pyrénées	the Pyrenees
les Alpes	the Alps
la Méditerranée	the Mediterranean

Dialogue

Mme Jones   Vous êtes né ici, monsieur?

M. Verriède   A Périgueux? Non, je suis né dans le département des Vosges, qui se trouve dans l'Est, et ma femme vient du Nord-Est, près de Strasbourg, en Alsace.

Mme Jones   Vous connaissez toutes les régions de France?

M. Verriède   Pas toutes. Il y en a 22, madame. Par exemple, je ne connais pas bien la Bretagne, dans l'Ouest. Mais toutes les régions du Midi, oui, plus ou moins.

Mme Jones   Le Midi? Qu'est-ce que c'est?

M. Verriède   C'est le Sud de la France. La moitié Sud, y compris l'Aquitaine, le Languedoc, la Provence – à mon avis, les plus belles régions de France, avec les Alpes, les Pyrénées et, bien sûr, la Méditerranée.

Exercices

1   **Ecoutez!**

Listen to these speakers saying where they are from. After each one, stop the recording if necessary, refer to the map on page 79 and tick the appropriate box. For example, the first comes from **Belfort**, which is in the East (**Est**) of France. (*Answers on page 127.*)

	NORD	SUD	EST	OUEST
Mme Clair	☐	☐	☐	☐
M. Simon	☐	☐	☐	☐
Mlle Drut	☐	☐	☐	☐
M. Monet	☐	☐	☐	☐

2 Lisez!
Vrai ou faux? Refer to the map of France on page 79 and the **En France** section. (*Answers on page 127.*)

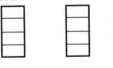

a) L'Alsace se trouve dans le sud-est de la France.
b) La Bretagne se trouve dans le Midi.
c) Un département est plus petit qu'une région.
d) Marseille se trouve en Provence.

3 ... et parlez français!
Answer the questions on the recording about where people come from, using the prompts below. First, play the part of an Englishman. (*Answers on pages 127–8.*)

1. Say 'Yes, I was born in Leeds, in the north'.
2. Say that your wife is French. She comes from Grasse, in Provence.
3. Say that you live in Bristol, in the west.

Now play the part of an American woman.

4. Say 'Yes, I was born in Miami, in the south'.
5. Say that you live in Philadelphia, in the east.

En français

1. 'To' or 'in' a town is **à** in French, e.g. **à Paris** – 'to/in Paris'. But use **en** to say 'in' or 'to' most European *countries and French regions*. (See Unit 21.)

> **en France/Angleterre/Aquitaine**   'in'/'to' France, etc.

2. *Points of the compass.* Note that the final consonants of **Su̱d** (South), **E̱st** (East) and **Ouest** (West) are pronounced. The final **d** of **Noṟd** (North), however, is silent.

3. *Reflexive verbs.* **Se trouver** is a common way of saying where a place is. **Qui se trouve** literally means 'which finds itself', in other words 'is situated'. You will meet more reflexive verbs in later units.

En France

France is divided into 22 **régions** and 95 **départements**.
   Just five regions are also known to English speakers by their English names: Brittany (**Bretagne**), Burgundy (**Bourgogne**), Normandy (**Normandie**), Picardy (**Picardie**) and the island of Corsica (**Corse**).
   The **départements** are numbered 1 to 95 in alphabetical order. This number appears as the last two digits on car registration plates and in the post code in addresses.

UNIT 25 Greetings and introductions

Adults and children

Vocabulaire

je vous présente	let me introduce you to
je vous en prie	please, please do
je vous apporte	I'll bring you
Comment tu t'appelles?	What's your name?
C'est ça?	Is that it?
Quel âge as-tu?	How old are you? (lit. What age have you?)
Tu as des frères ou des sœurs?	Do you have any brothers or sisters?
ta maman	your mother/mum
avec elle	with her
à la maison	at home
ma sœur aînée	my elder sister
asseyez-vous	sit down
quelque chose à boire	something to drink

Dialogue

(Mr and Mrs Jones are on holiday with their son Daniel ...)

Mrs Jones	Je vous présente mon mari, Peter.
Mme Martin	Enchantée, monsieur.
Mrs Jones	Et notre fils.
Daniel Jones	Bonjour, madame.
Mme Martin	Bonjour! Comment tu t'appelles?
Daniel	Je m'appelle Daniel.
Mme Martin	Mais tu parles très bien! Ta maman est française, et tu parles français avec elle à la maison, c'est ça?
Daniel	Oui.
Mme Martin	Et quel âge as-tu, Daniel?
Daniel	J'ai treize ans, madame.
Mme Martin	Tu as des frères ou des sœurs?
Daniel	J'ai une sœur aînée, elle s'appelle Sally. Elle a dix-sept ans.
Mrs Jones	Mais asseyez-vous, je vous en prie, Madame Martin. Je vous apporte quelque chose à boire.

Exercices

1 Ecoutez!

Listen to the recording of a Frenchwoman talking about herself and her family and supply the missing details below. (Refer back to Unit 17 for this exercise and for Exercise 3.) (*Answers on page 128.*)

a) Name   <u>Nicole Fournier</u>
    Age   _____
    Born in   _____
    Resident in   _____
    Present job   _____

b) Name   <u>Marie Staub</u>
    Age   _____
    Resident in   _____
    No. of children   _____
    Present job   _____

2 Lisez!

Match the halves of these sentences. (*Answers on page 128.*)

a) Asseyez-vous,   i)   mon mari, Peter
b) Tu as des frères   ii) je vous en prie
c) Comment   iii) quelque chose à boire
d) Je vous présente   iv) ou des sœurs?
e) Je vous apporte   v)   tu t'appelles?

3 … et parlez français!

In the conversation you take the part of 15-year-old Jean-Pierre from Grenoble. Answer questions about yourself and your 21-year-old sister Sabine who is a teacher. (*Answers on page 128.*)

En français

1. The **tu** form of the verb in the present tense usually ends in a silent **-s** and sounds the same as the form for **je**.

> **Je parl<u>e</u>, tu parl<u>es</u>   Je prend<u>s</u>, tu prend<u>s</u>   J'habit<u>e</u>, tu habit<u>es</u>**

In just a few cases **je** and **tu** have distinct forms.

> **Je <u>suis</u>, tu <u>es</u>   J'<u>ai</u>, tu <u>as</u>   Je <u>vais</u>, tu <u>vas</u>**

2. **Avoir** and **être**. Listen after Exercise 3 to the present tense of these two irregular verbs. It is very important that you know all the forms by heart.

3. The phrase **Je vous en prie** appears again (see Unit 7), this time with the meaning 'Please do'.

En France

Tu is used for 'you' when addressing children, close friends and members of the family. It is commonly used in preference to the more formal **vous** amongst young people, but as an adult you should wait until a French person changes from **vous** to **tu** before doing so yourself. **Vous** must always be used when addressing more than one person, even friends and family. Also bear in mind that the French shake hands each time they meet, and not just on first acquaintance as in England.

UNIT 26 In the café

The café-tabac

Vocabulaire

un chocolat chaud	a hot chocolate
au fond	at the back
avec les journaux	with the newspapers
Attends-moi	Wait for me
chéri	darling
je vais téléphoner (à)	I'm going to telephone (to)
en attendant	while (I'm) waiting
une télécarte	a phone card
au sous-sol	in the basement

Dialogue

Waitress	Bonjour, messieurs-dames!
Paul Ravel	Bonjour! Un chocolat chaud et un café au lait, s'il vous plaît.
Waitress	Voilà, messieurs-dames …
Julie Ravel	Non, le café c'est pour moi. Merci. Mademoiselle, est-ce que vous avez des cartes postales?
Waitress	Oui, madame. Au fond, avec les journaux.
Julie Ravel	Ah oui, je vois. Attends-moi, chéri.
Paul Ravel	Julie, je vais téléphoner à Marcel en attendant. Mademoiselle, une télécarte, s'il vous plaît.
Waitress	Pour vingt francs? Voilà, monsieur. Les téléphones sont au sous-sol.

Télécartes en vente ici
Télécartes on sale here

Exercices

1 Ecoutez!

Listen to this conversation and circle the correct answer. (*Answers on page 128.*)

a) Who is the coffee for? — Brigitte / Georges
b) What other drink is ordered? — tea / chocolate
c) What sandwiches are ordered? — ham / cheese
d) How much is the bill? — 29F40 / 39F40
e) Where is the telephone? — in the basement / at the back

2 Lisez! Ecrivez!

Use the words below to complete the sentences. (*Answers on page 128.*)

sous-sol   chéri   chaud   vais   attendant   lait   téléphones

a) Un chocolat _____ et un café au _____ .
b) Je _____ téléphoner à l'hôtel en _____ .
c) Attends-moi, _____ .
d) Les _____ sont au _____ .

3 … et parlez français!

Use the prompts below to order drinks and make a telephone call. (*Answers on page 128.*)

1. Order a draught beer and a (freshly squeezed) orange juice.
2. And three postcards.
3. Ask 'Where is the telephone, please?'
4. Finally, say 'I'd like a phone card for 20 francs.'

En français

1. *The future.* To talk about what you are *going* to do – just say as in English:

Je vais téléphoner	I am going to phone
Je vais acheter	I am going to buy

Learn all the forms of **aller** (on your recording after Exercise 3 and in the Verb Tables on pages 131–2) so that you can say 'We are going to …', 'They are going to …' etc.

e.g.	**Nous allons téléphoner**	We are going to telephone
	Ils vont acheter	They are going to buy

2. Most nouns and adjectives in **-al** change to **-aux** in the plural.

le journal	les journaux

En France

French cafés are as much bars as cafés and stay open till late in the evening. All are licensed to sell alcoholic, as well as soft drinks. In a **café-tabac** – often displaying the sign 'T' outside – you will also usually be able to buy postage stamps, telephone cards, even bus tickets.

At the hotel

Confirming a reservation

Vocabulaire

confirmer	to confirm
A quel nom?	In what name?
Je l'épelle	I'll spell it
j'ai téléphoné	I telephoned
la semaine dernière	last week
un instant	one moment
Je vais vérifier	I'll check
une chambre à deux lits	a twin-bedded room
du 15 au 17 avril	from the 15th to the 17th of April
A demain	See you tomorrow
j'espère	I hope
noté	noted
sortie	exit
direction Laplume	(going) to Laplume
sur la droite	on the right
vieux	old
château	chateau, castle
Bonne route!	Have a safe journey!

Dialogue

Receptionist	Allô! Hôtel Bellevue.
Tourist	Je voudrais confirmer une réservation pour demain, s'il vous plaît.
Receptionist	Oui, madame. C'est à quel nom?
Tourist	Willoughby. Je l'épelle. W I L L O U G H B Y. J'ai téléphoné la semaine dernière.
Receptionist	Un instant, madame. Je vais vérifier … Oui, Willoughby. Une chambre à deux lits. Du quinze au dix-sept avril. C'est noté, madame. Vous arrivez à quelle heure?
Tourist	Vers sept heures, j'espère. Euh, est-ce que je quitte l'autoroute à Agen?
Receptionist	Oui, c'est ça. Sortie numéro 7. Puis vous prenez la N 931, direction Laplume – L A P L U M E – et l'hôtel se trouve à deux kilomètres sur la droite, juste après le vieux château.
Tourist	Merci beaucoup, monsieur.
Receptionist	Je vous en prie, madame. A demain et bonne route!

Exercices

1 Ecoutez!

Listen to the French alphabet, referring to the **En français** section opposite. Then try the exercise, completing the well-known place-names you hear spelt out on your recording. (*Answers on page 128.*)

C _ _ _ _ _   P _ _ _ _   M _ _ _ _ _ _ _ _
N _ _   _ _ _ _   B _ _ _ _ _ _ _

2 Lisez! Ecrivez!

Familiarize yourself with the dialogue by listening to it and reading it several times, then cover up the text and see if you can fill in the missing words in the extract below.

Receptionist	Un instant madame. Je vais _____ . Oui, Willoughby. Une _____ à deux _____ , du quinze ___ dix-sept avril. C'est noté, madame. Vous _____ à _____ heure?
Tourist	Vers sept _____ , j'espère. Est-ce que je _____ l'autoroute à Agen?
Receptionist	Oui, c'est ça. _____ numéro 7. Puis vous _____ la N 931, _____ Laplume.

3 ... et parlez français!

Use the name 'Jenkins' and telephone the **Hôtel de la Plage** to confirm your bookings – a double room for 3 days from April 19th. The receptionist answers the phone. (*Answers on page 128.*)

1. I would like to confirm a reservation.
2. My name is Jenkins. I'll spell it. J E N K I N S.
3. Yes, that's it. I telephoned on Monday.
4. About six o'clock.

En français

1. *The perfect tense* – for past events. Another example of the perfect tense in this unit: **J'ai téléphoné**. Make sure you know the present tense endings of **avoir** – you will then be able to say:

J'ai téléphoné	I phoned	**Nous avons téléphoné**	We phoned
Tu as parlé	You spoke	**Vous avez travaillé**	You worked
Il/elle a acheté	He/she bought	**Ils/elles ont donné**	They gave

The above can also mean 'I *have* phoned', 'You *have* spoken', etc.

2. *The alphabet.* To spell a word to a French person you will need to know the French names of the letters in the alphabet. Listen to the alphabet on your recording after Exercise 3. For double letters say **deux** followed by the letter, e.g. 'double t' is **deux t**. 'How do you spell it?' is **Comment ça s'épelle?** or **Comment ça s'écrit?**

3. *Dates.* 'The fifteenth of April' in French is simply **le quinze avril** and 'from the 15th to the 17th' is **du quinze au dix-sept**. But 'the *first* of April' is **le premier avril**.

En France

Hotels – most will reserve a room by telephone, so it will help if you can spell your name in French and take down a French place-name accurately if one is dictated to you.
Roads – Road numbers are preceded by the letter **A** for **Autoroute** (motorway), **N** for **Nationale** (major road) and **D** for **Départementale** (minor road).

 **Numbers**

Arranging to meet

Vocabulaire

Salut!	Hi!, Hello!
Ça va?	How are you?
si tu veux	if you want
finalement	finally
eh bien	let's see
tu la connais	you know her
qui partage	who shares
un studio	a bed-sit
au-dessus de la pâtisserie	above the cake-shop
Quelle mémoire!	What a memory!
je me souviens	I remember
rendez-vous	meeting
la gare routière	the bus station
le car part	the coach leaves
entendu	understood, agreed
Ciao!	Bye!

Dialogue

Henri	Salut, Sylvie! Ça va?
Sylvie	Salut! Alors, tu viens demain, Henri?
Henri	Oui, si tu veux. Vous êtes combien finalement?
Sylvie	Eh bien, nous sommes quatre. Il y a toi et moi, puis Jean-Marc et Anne-Marie …
Henri	Anne-Marie?
Sylvie	Tu la connais – la petite blonde qui partage un studio avec Sandrine. Mais quelle mémoire! Rue Balzac. Dans le onzième, au-dessus de la pâtisserie.
Henri	Oh oui, je me souviens. Alors bon, d'accord.
Sylvie	Alors rendez-vous à la gare routière vers huit heures et quart, huit heures et demie. Le car part à neuf heures moins le quart.
Henri	Entendu. A demain. Huit heures et demie. Ciao!

Exercices

1 **Ecoutez!**

Read the **En français** section 1 carefully, then listen to the times and mark in the hands on the clock faces. (*Answers on page 128.*)

2 Lisez! Ecrivez!
Convert the following 24-hour times to the 12-hour system. The first is done for you. (*Answers on page 128.*)

a) 13h50   Deux heures moins dix
b) 17h20   _____
c) 18h15   _____
d) 20h30   _____
e) 23h45   _____

3 … et parlez français!
Read aloud the times you have drawn on the clock faces in Exercise 1. Check your answers on the recording.

En français

1. The twelve-hour clock is revised in this unit. To express 'a.m.' and 'p.m.' in French, say **du matin** and **du soir**. You can also add **de l'après-midi** – 'of the afternoon' for between midday and five o'clock.

> **Trois heures de l'après-midi**   3 p.m.

Also useful to know: 'half an hour' is **une demi-heure**; 'a quarter of an hour' is **un quart d'heure**.

2. Note 'There are two of us' is simply 'We are two' – **Nous sommes deux**.

3. In the phrase **dans le onzième** – 'in the 11th district' – note that **le** does not abbreviate to **l'** before the word **onzième**.

4. *Adverbs.* Adding **-ment** to the feminine form of an adjective will usually give you the adverb.

> **lent*ement***   slow*ly*   **final*ement***   final*ly*

En France

Amongst friends who are using **tu** the language will obviously be more informal in a number of ways, and **Salut!** is likely to replace **Bonjour!** as a greeting. The Italian **Ciao** is also popular with young people. **Ça va?** is an informal 'How are you?' 'How's things?' And a friendly kiss on both cheeks, not just a handshake, is the rule. Remember **tu** is only used when addressing one person. If you are talking to more than one person, even informally, you must use **vous**.

Talking about yourself

Hobbies and sports

Vocabulaire

nager	to swim
sortir	to go out
danser	to dance
je joue au tennis	I play tennis
j'adore	I love
je déteste	I hate
Ma femme fait	My wife does
de la gymnastique	gymnastics
Daniel fait du vélo	Daniel does cycling
la piscine	the swimming pool
centre de loisirs	leisure centre
une discothèque	a discotheque
mes copains (fem. **copines**)	my friends, schoolfriends
ton sport préféré	your favourite sport
paresseux (fem. **paresseuse**)	lazy
voilà	there you are
tous les samedis	every Saturday
de temps en temps	from time to time
très mal	very badly
une bonne idée	a good idea
Super!	Great!

Dialogue

Claire Vous aimez le sport, Monsieur Jones?

M. Jones Moi, je suis assez paresseux. Je joue au tennis de temps en temps, mais très mal. Ma femme fait de la gymnastique et notre fils Daniel fait du vélo. Il aime beaucoup nager, il va tous les dimanches à la piscine municipale. Puis notre fille … euh … Quel est ton sport préféré, Sally?

Sally Moi, je déteste les sports. Je préfère sortir avec mes copains. J'adore danser, voilà, c'est mon sport préféré.

Claire Ecoutez. Au centre de loisirs il y a une discothèque tous les samedis en été.

Sally Une disco? Super!

M. Jones C'est une bonne idée.

Exercices

1 **Ecoutez!**

Listen to Stéphanie and Patrick talking about their interests and mark the boxes **VRAI** and **FAUX**. (*Answers on page 128.*)

Stéphanie's favourite sport is squash.
She goes swimming twice a week.
Her friend Brigitte loves dancing.
Patrick never does any gymnastics.
He prefers TV to badminton.

VRAI	FAUX

2   Lisez! Ecrivez!

Refer to the vocabulary in the **En France** and **En français** sections then complete the missing words in this text. (*Answers on page 128.*)

J'aime beaucoup nager. C'est mon sport p _ _ _ _ _ é. Je vais à la p _ _ _ _ _ e
tous les s _ _ _ _ _ s. Mon frère est très p _ _ _ _ _ _ _ _ x, il d _ _ _ _ _ e tous
les sports, mais il j _ _ e très bien de la g _ _ _ _ _ e et va tous les
v _ _ _ _ _ _ _ s d _ _ _ _ r à la discothèque avec ses c _ _ _ _ _ s.

3   … et parlez français!

You are asked about your leisure activities. Answer the questions using the prompts below. (*Answers on page 128.*)

When asked about:
tennis – Say you like tennis very much.
gymnastics – No, you don't like gymnastics, you hate gymnastics.
piano – Yes, you like to play the piano.
going out – You like very much going out with your friends.

En français

faire and *jouer*

1.   Use **jouer à** for games and **jouer de** for musical instruments.

> **Je joue au tennis** (masc.)   **Je joue du piano** (masc.)
> **à la pétanque** (fem.)   **de la guitare** (fem.)

2.   Learn the forms of the irregular verb **faire** (in the Verb Tables on pages 131–2 and on your recording after Exercise 3). In the dialogue you met **Ma femme fait** – 'My wife does' and in Exercise 1 **Je fais** – 'I do'. Remember that **faire** is also used to mean 'to make', e.g. **Ça fait 10 francs** – 'That makes 10 francs.'

En France

Many sports keep the English name, e.g. **le football**, **le hockey**, **le golf**, **le tennis** and are masculine. Swimming and horse-riding are **la natation** and **l'équitation**. You can do skiing – **faire du ski** at **une station de ski** – ski resort, while on a hot summer afternoon a gentle game of **boules** or **pétanque**, the French versions of bowls, is a common sight on the village squares of France. Incidentally, those mysterious signs pointing to **Ball Trap** which you may see while driving along country roads in France, mean clay pigeon shooting.

Out and about

The weather

Vocabulaire

Quel temps fait-il?	What's the weather like?
Il fait beau	It's fine (weather)
Il fait mauvais	The weather is bad
Il fait chaud	It's hot
Il fait froid	It's cold
Il pleut	It's raining
la boulangerie	the baker's
en face de l'église	opposite the church
Vous allez vous promener?	Are you going for a walk?
Il y en a une	There is one (of them)
à deux cents mètres	two hundred metres away
Pourquoi sortir la voiture?	Why get the car out?
Laissez votre voiture	Leave your car
Il ne va pas pleuvoir	It's not going to rain
Vous croyez?	Do you think so?
le ciel	the sky
comme il est clair	how clear it is
pas un nuage	not a cloud
chez vous	in your country
je viens de téléphoner	I have just telephoned
Bonne promenade!	Have a good walk!

Dialogue

M. Verriède	Ah, bonjour, Madame Jones!
Mrs Jones	Bonjour, Monsieur Verriède. Il fait chaud aujourd'hui.
M. Verriède	Oui, oui. Il fait beau. Vous allez vous promener?
Mrs Jones	Non, je vais à la boulangerie.
M. Verriède	Il ne faut pas aller jusqu'au centre. Il y en a une à deux cents mètres, en face de l'église. Pourquoi sortir la voiture? Laissez votre voiture dans le garage, madame. Il ne va pas pleuvoir aujourd'hui.
Mrs Jones	Vous croyez?
M. Verriède	Regardez le ciel comme il est clair, pas un nuage! Ici, ce n'est pas l'Angleterre! Quel temps fait-il chez vous?
Mrs Jones	En Angleterre? Je viens de téléphoner. Il fait mauvais. Il pleut et il fait froid!
M. Verriède	Ah! Alors bonne promenade, madame!

Exercices

1 **Ecoutez!**

Now see if you can understand a French weather forecast. Will it be **beau temps** – 'fine weather' – in all the four cities mentioned? Listen to the forecast – **la météo** – and tick the boxes appropriately at the top of the next page. Note the expressions **vents froids** – 'cold winds', and **orages** – 'storms'. (*Answers on page 128.*)

City					
Paris					
Rouen					
Grenoble					
Perpignan					

2 Lisez!

Match the halves of these phrases taken from the dialogue. (*Answers on page 128.*)

a) Il y en a une   i) comme il est clair
b) Il ne va pas   ii) de téléphoner
c) Regardez le ciel   iii) jusqu'au centre
d) Je viens   iv) à deux cents mètres
e) Il ne faut pas aller   v) pleuvoir aujourd'hui

3 … et parlez français!

You're asked about the weather back home. You've just heard it's atrocious so give your French friends as much detail as you can. Use the prompts. (*Answers on page 128.*)

1. No, the weather is bad.
2. Say that you have just phoned.
3. Yes, it's raining.
4. No, it's very cold.

En français

1. *The weather*. The verb **faire** is used for many everyday expressions about the weather. You may also find the following useful:

Il fait doux	It's mild
Il fait du vent	It's windy
Il fait du brouillard	It's foggy

But note there are special verbs for 'to rain' – **pleuvoir** and 'to snow' – **neiger**.
Faire is not used in these expressions.

Il pleut	It's raining	**Il neige**	It's snowing

2. The verb **venir** + **de** means 'to have just' done something.

Je <u>viens de</u> téléphoner	I have just phoned
Le train <u>vient d'arriver</u>	The train has just arrived

Venir is an irregular verb. You will find it in the Verb Tables on page 132 and on your recording after Exercise 3.

En France

France has an extremely varied climate and the weather is always a popular topic of conversation. So for the foreign tourist there is no better way of eliciting a smile and a friendly exchange with the natives after your opening **Bonjour!** than with a friendly **Il fait beau! Il fait froid!** or simply **Quel temps!** – 'What weather!'

 **Public transport**

The Paris Metro

Vocabulaire

la Tour Eiffel	the Eiffel Tower
je peux vous donner	I can give you
un carnet de dix tickets	a book of ten tickets
ou bien	or else
le réseau	the network
le métro	the tube/underground
ça revient	it works out, costs
pendant quelques jours	for several days

Dialogue

Ticket clerk	Mademoiselle?
Tourist	C'est quelle direction pour aller à la Tour Eiffel, s'il vous plaît?
Ticket clerk	Porte de la Chapelle. Puis changez à Pasteur et prenez la direction Charles de Gaulle.
Tourist	Merci. Deux tickets, s'il vous plaît. Aller-retour.
Ticket clerk	Aller-retour? Il n'y a pas d'aller-retour pour le métro, mademoiselle. Je peux vous donner quatre tickets à 9F ou un carnet de dix tickets pour 48F. Ou bien une carte 'Paris Visite'.
Tourist	'Paris-Visite'? Qu'est-ce que c'est?
Ticket clerk	C'est valable pendant 3 ou 5 jours et pour tout le réseau RATP – métro et autobus. Ça revient moins cher si vous êtes à Paris pendant quelques jours. C'est 95F pour 3 jours et 150F pour 5 jours.
Tourist	C'est une bonne idée. Alors deux, s'il vous plaît. Pour trois jours.
Ticket clerk	Ça fait 190F, s'il vous plaît, mademoiselle.

Exercices

1 Ecoutez!

Listen as a tourist buys a Paris metro ticket. Are the following details true or false? (Refer to the **En France** section.) (*Answers on page 128.*)

	VRAI	FAUX
a) The tourist buys a 5-day **Paris Visite** card.		
b) Her travel card costs 250F.		
c) Her destination is **Château de Vincennes**.		
d) She is told to change at **Châtelet**.		

2 Lisez!

Read the dialogue again and answer these questions in English. (*Answers on page 128.*)

a) What is the price of a single ticket? _____
b) How much is a book of ten tickets? _____
c) How much is a 5-day travel card? _____
d) Where on the RATP network can it be used, apart from on the tube? _____

3 ... et parlez français!

Listen again to the dialogue. Stop the recording as necessary and take the part of the tourist. Check your answers on the recording.

1.   Ask 'What direction to go to the Tour Eiffel station, please?'
2.   The ticket clerk gives you directions. Thank him and ask for two return tickets.
3.   He suggests a Paris-Visite ticket. Ask 'Paris-Visite? What's that?'
4.   He explains the Paris-Visite card. Say it's a good idea, then ask for two, for three days.

En français

| **Quel(le)?** | **Qu'est-ce que?** |

You will have noticed two distinct ways of asking 'What' in the units so far.

a) **Quel(le)** is nearly always followed immediately by a *noun*.

Quelle <u>heure</u> est-il?	What time is it?
Quel <u>temps</u> fait-il?	What is the weather like?
C'est quelle <u>direction</u>?	What line is it?

b) **Qu'est-ce que**, on the other hand, usually introduces a *verb*.

| **Qu'est-ce que <u>vous voulez</u>?** | What do you want? |
| **Qu'est-ce que <u>c'est</u>?** | What is it? What's that? |

En France

The **Paris Visite** card gives unlimited travel on the **RATP (Régie Autonome des Transports Parisiens)** within the Greater Paris area. You can also use it on the **RER (Réseau Express Régional)** for fast, cross-Paris and suburban journeys.

Two points to remember:
(i)   The Paris metro uses a flat rate fare system for any length of trip in central Paris.
(ii)   Metro lines are not given names and there are no signs such as 'Northbound' so always check the **Direction** signs for the name of the final station on your line and you will not get lost!

Shopping

At the department store

Vocabulaire

cette jupe	this skirt
ce chemisier	this blouse
cette robe blanche	this white dress
Vous l'avez	You have it
en d'autres couleurs?	in other colours?
jaune	yellow
bleu clair	light blue
rose	pink
Quelle taille faites-vous?	What size are you?
la taille au-dessus	the size above/next size
je fais du 38	I'm a 38
Je peux essayer la rose?	Can I try the pink?
le salon d'essayage	the fitting room
Je vous l'apporte	I'll bring it to you
La couleur vous va	The colour suits you

Dialogue

Assistant	Je peux vous aider, madame?
Customer	Oui, alors cette jupe et ce chemisier, s'il vous plaît, et puis encore cette robe blanche, vous l'avez en d'autres couleurs?
Assistant	Celle-ci, madame? Oui, nous l'avons en jaune, en bleu clair et en rose. Quelle taille faites-vous?
Customer	Je fais du 38. Elle coûte combien?
Assistant	260F, madame.
Customer	Je peux essayer la rose, s'il vous plaît?
Assistant	Bien sûr. Le salon d'essayage est là-bas, madame …
Customer	… Dommage! Elle est trop petite. Avez-vous la taille au-dessus?
Assistant	Je vous l'apporte tout de suite, madame …
Assistant	… La couleur vous va très bien, madame.
Customer	Oui, elle me plaît beaucoup. Je la prends.

Exercices

1 Ecoutez!

Listen and ring round the correct detail. (*Answers on page 128.*)

The customer wants to try on a *dress/skirt/blouse*. She can have *red/white/blue/black*. She chooses *red/white/blue* and goes to try it on in the fitting room *on the right/on the left/at the back*. Her size is *36/38/40*, but the one she is given is too *big/small*. She eventually finds the right size and buys it together with a *dress/skirt/blouse* and pays *450F/500F/550F* by *cheque/credit card/travellers' cheque*.

2 Lisez! Ecrivez!

Can you find *nine* words, to do with buying clothes, written vertically or horizontally in the wordsquare below? (*Answers on page 128*.)

V	L	A	C	J	E	C	L	A	I	R
E	T	I	H	U	B	L	E	U	X	O
R	O	S	E	P	R	E	Z	D	Y	B
T	R	E	R	E	G	R	P	I	U	E
B	L	A	N	C	O	U	L	E	U	R

3 ... et parlez français!

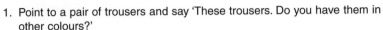

Re-enact the dialogue. Buy yourself a pair of trousers in the department store. Bear in mind the French refer to 'a trouser' – **un pantalon** – in the singular, not 'trousers' as in English. (*Answers on page 128*.) The assistant starts by asking if she can help you.

1. Point to a pair of trousers and say 'These trousers. Do you have them in other colours?'
2. Tell her your size and ask how much they cost.
3. Ask 'Can I try the blue?'
4. Say 'A pity. They're too small.' Ask 'Do you have the size above?'
5. Say 'Yes, I like them. I'll take them.'

En français

1. *Adjectives.* Note these examples:

un pantalon <u>rouge</u>	un pullover <u>vert</u>	un chemisier <u>blanc</u>
une jupe <u>rouge</u>	une robe <u>verte</u>	une jupe <u>blanche</u>

   a) All *adjectives of colour* come *after* the noun.
   b) Remember adjectives ending in **-e**, e.g. **rouge**, **jaune**, do not change for the feminine form.
   c) The adjective **blanc** has an irregular feminine form: **blanche**.

2. Remember from Unit 15 – *object pronouns* **le**, **la**, **les** *precede* the verb.

Vous l'avez?   Do you have it?   **Je la prends**   I'll take it

Two object pronouns appear together before the verb in the example **Je vous l'apporte** – 'I'll bring *it to you*.'

En France

Department stores – such as **Galeries Lafayette** and **Au Printemps** – are called simply **grands magasins** – 'large shops'. Look out for the sign in the windows saying **SOLDES**, meaning 'Sales'. If you are looking for shoes – **chaussures** – the word for size is not **taille** but **pointure**. Finally, bear in mind French sizes for shoes and clothing are different!

UNIT 33 — Services

At the doctor's

Vocabulaire

Qu'est-ce qui ne va pas?	What's the matter?
j'ai mal	I've got a pain/ache
je suis malade	I'm ill
ventre	stomach
dos	back
tête	head
gorge	throat
dents	teeth
yeux	eyes
fièvre	fever
température	temperature
grippe	flu
hier	yesterday
verre	glass
comprimés	tablets
pilule	pill
trois fois par jour	three times a day
après les repas	after meals
je crois	I think so
rien de très grave	nothing very serious
si ça ne va pas mieux	if it's not better
revenez	come back
docteur	doctor

Dialogue

Doctor	Qu'est-ce qui ne va pas, monsieur?
Patient	J'ai très mal au ventre depuis hier soir.
Doctor	Vous avez de la fièvre?
Patient	Oui, je crois.
Doctor	Asseyez-vous, monsieur. Je vais prendre votre température. Oui, 37°5. Rien de très grave. Qu'est-ce que vous avez mangé hier?
Patient	Des salades, une pizza et trois verres de vin.
Doctor	C'est peut-être ça. Alors je vais vous donner des comprimés. Vous allez les prendre trois fois par jour après les repas. Si ça ne va pas mieux, revenez jeudi.
Patient	Merci beaucoup. Au revoir, docteur.

Exercices

1 Ecoutez!

Listen to two consultations at the doctor's surgery and note down the details in the boxes at the top of the next page. (*Answers on page 128.*)

Patient	Symptoms	Prescription	Dose	Further details, appointments
A				
B				

Did you hear which patient had the flu (**la grippe**)?

2 Lisez! Ecrivez!
Use the words on the right to complete these statements about various
common ailments. (*Answers on page 128.*)

a) J'ai mal à la _____   ventre
b) J'ai de la _____   dents
c) Je vais prendre des _____   repas
d) J'ai mal au _____   comprimés
e) J'ai mal aux _____   fièvre
f) Je vais prendre une pilule après les _____   gorge

3 … et parlez français!
Using the recording from Exercise 1, stop the tape as necessary to speak the
parts of patients A and B. Check your answers on the recording.

En français

1. Note how the forms **au**, **à la** and **aux** (Unit 14) are used with **AVOIR** to say that
something is wrong with you.

	au ventre	(masc.)		stomach ache
J'ai mal	**à la tête**	(fem.)	I have	a headache
	aux dents	(plural)		toothache

2. Two ways of saying 'What?'

Unit 31 { **Qu'est-ce qui ne va pas?** 'What' is the *subject* of **va**.
Unit 33 { **Qu'est-ce que vous voulez?** 'What' is the *object* of **voulez**. ('You' is
the subject.)

En France

In France both doctors' fees and medicines (**médicaments**) prescribed must be
paid for at the time of treatment though EU citizens may claim back around 75%
of costs. After the consultation the prescription (**l'ordonnance**) must be taken to
the **pharmacie** (chemist's). The price label (**la vignette**) is detached from the
medicine and affixed to the **feuille de maladie** (illness certificate) which is handed
in later for reimbursement.

34 Eating out

Main courses

Vocabulaire

plat principal	main dish
tellement	so much, all that much
entrecôte	rib steak
à la niçoise	'Nice' style
une tranche	a slice
garnie d'anchois	served with anchovies
poulet rôti	roast chicken
légumes	vegetables
haricots verts	green beans
pommes frites	fried potatoes, chips
petits pois	peas
carottes	carrots
eau minérale	mineral water

Dialogue

Waitress	Qu'est-ce que vous prenez comme plat principal? Vous avez décidé?
Madame Duval	Je ne sais pas. Je n'aime pas tellement le poisson. Entrecôte à la niçoise, qu'est-ce que c'est?
Waitress	C'est une tranche d'entrecôte au vin blanc, garnie d'anchois et d'olives.
Madame Duval	C'est d'accord. L'entrecôte pour moi.
Waitress	Et pour monsieur?
Monsieur Duval	Moi, je préfère le poulet rôti.
Waitress	Qu'est-ce que vous désirez comme légumes – petits pois, carottes, haricots verts?
Monsieur Duval	Chérie? Des haricots verts? Oui? ... Et des pommes frites, s'il vous plaît.
Waitress	Et comme boisson?
Monsieur Duval	Une bouteille de St Emilion.
Madame Duval	Et un verre d'eau minérale pour moi.

Exercices

1   Ecoutez!

Listen to the waiter explaining three dishes from the menu and tick the appropriate boxes as you hear the ingredients mentioned. (*Answers on page 128.*)

A									
B									
C									

2 Lisez!

These two menus seem to have been written by a drunken waiter – see if you can unscramble the words to produce some edible dishes! For example, the first item should be: **Salade mixte**.

3 ... et parlez français!

Now use the prompts to order a meal for two people in a French restaurant. (*Answers on page 128.*)

1. Order a green salad and mixed shellfish.
2. You want to check an item on the menu – **coq au vin**. Ask what it is.
3. Say you don't like chicken all that much. Order one fillet of sole and one steak with chips.
4. Order a carafe of white wine and a glass of mineral water.

En français

Past participles like **grillé**, **rôti**, **servi**, **garni** to say 'grilled', 'roasted', 'served', 'accompanied', will all have an extra **e** or **s** is they go with something feminine or plural, e.g. **entrecôte grillée**. Use **garni** to ask if the dishes are 'garnished', i.e. served with vegetables: **Les plats sont garnis?**

En France

Restaurants will often offer a reasonably priced **menu touristique** and a **menu gastronomique** starting from around 100 francs. Also look out for the **menu enfants** – 'children's menu'.

Some of the other popular regional dishes you might try are: **coq au vin** – chicken cooked in wine, **choucroute garnie**, from Alsace – sauerkraut with sausage and pork, cooked in white wine, **cassoulet** – a bean casserole from the Pyrenees region, and **gratin dauphinois** – a popular cheese dish from the South-East of France.

35 Travel by car

Breakdown

Vocabulaire

service dépannage	breakdown service
je suis en panne	I've broken down
Quel est le problème?	What is the problem?
l'embrayage	the clutch
la boîte de vitesses	the gearbox
changer de vitesse	to change gear
la marque	the make
le modèle	the model
votre véhicule	your vehicle
l'année de fabrication	the year of manufacture
le numéro d'immatriculation	the registration number
Combien de temps faut-il attendre?	How long must I wait?
environ	about

Dialogue

Employee	Allô! Service dépannage. Je peux vous aider?
Motorist	Oui, je suis en panne.
Employee	Vous êtes où, monsieur?
Motorist	Je suis devant l'Hôtel du Midi, sur la N7 près de Tourves. Direction St Maximin.
Employee	Et votre nom, s'il vous plaît?
Motorist	Moreau.
Employee	Quel est le problème, Monsieur Moreau?
Motorist	Je ne sais pas si c'est l'embrayage ou la boîte de vitesses. Je ne peux pas changer de vitesse.
Employee	La marque et le modèle de votre véhicule, monsieur?
Motorist	C'est une Renault Espace.
Employee	Quelle couleur?
Motorist	Bleue.
Employee	L'année de fabrication?
Motorist	95.
Employee	Et le numéro d'immatriculation?
Motorist	303 OR 95. Combien de temps faut-il attendre, madame?
Employee	Environ une demi-heure, monsieur.

Exercices

1 Ecoutez!

Listen to another motorist reporting a breakdown and note down the details she gives. Refer back to Unit 27 to refresh your memory with the letters of the alphabet. (*Answers on page 128.*)

Location	_____
Problem	_____
Make of car	_____
Model	_____

Colour	_____
Year	_____
Motorist's name	_____

2 Lisez!

Match the following questions with their answers. (*Answers on page 128.*)

a) Où êtes-vous?

b) Quelle couleur?

c) Je peux vous aider?

d) Combien de temps faut-il attendre?

e) Et l'année de fabrication?

f) Quel est le problème, monsieur?

g) Quelle est la marque de votre véhicule?

i) 1993

ii) C'est une Citroën

iii) Rouge

iv) Devant l'Hôtel du Midi

v) Oui, je suis en panne

vi) Environ une demi-heure

vii) Je ne peux pas changer de vitesse

3 ... et parlez français!

You've broken down. Stay calm! And phone the breakdown service for assistance. The prompts below tell you what details to give. (*Answers on page 128.*)

1. Say that you've broken down. You're in front of the **Hôtel Splendide** in Avallon.
2. Say you don't know. You think it's the clutch.
3. It's a Renault 16.
4. Black.
5. 94.

En français

1. If you remember the expression **Il faut** – 'It's necessary, I/We/You, etc. must/have to/need', then you will recognize **Faut-il?** as the form often used after question words like **Combien? Où?** etc.

Combien de temps faut-il attendre?	How long must I wait?
Où faut-il aller?	Where must I go?

2. Note that all makes of vehicle are feminine. So the French refer to **une Peugeot, une Renault, ma Citroën, ma Mondéo**, etc.

En France

In Belgium and Switzerland the **Touring Club Royal de Belgique** (**TCB**) and **Touring Club Suisse** (**TCS**) both operate breakdown services. Your Continental motoring policy will entitle you to call on them if you break down on holiday. In France, however, there is no national equivalent and you should telephone the nearest **service dépannage** and arrange for them to **réparer** (repair) your car or **remorquer** (tow) it to the nearest garage.

 **Talking about France**

The regions of France

Vocabulaire

le meilleur climat	the best climate
la meilleure cuisine	the best cuisine, the best food
en hiver	in winter
en été	in summer
il fait doux	it's mild
la côte	the coast
la Côte d'Azur	the Côte d'Azur, the Riviera
la mer	the sea
le paysage	the scenery
la montagne	the mountain(s)
les plages	the beaches
sont magnifiques	are magnificent
calme	calm
pollué	polluted
on trouve	one finds
surtout	everywhere
peut-être	perhaps

Dialogue

Christiane	Quelle est votre région préférée de France?
Bernard	Moi, je préfère la Provence parce que la Provence a le meilleur climat. Même en hiver il fait doux sur la Côte d'Azur. Puis en Provence vous avez tout – le soleil, la mer et la montagne.
Chantal	J'aime beaucoup la Provence, mais je préfère la Bretagne en été. Surtout pour les enfants; les plages sont magnifiques.
Christiane	Pour moi, la plus belle région c'est l'Auvergne. Le paysage est très, très beau. C'est plus calme que sur la côte et c'est beaucoup moins pollué. Il y a de la bonne cuisine aussi et c'est moins cher.
Bernard	Mais si vous aimez la bonne cuisine – c'est en Bourgogne qu'on trouve la meilleure cuisine de France, et peut-être aussi les meilleurs vins.

Exercices

1   Ecoutez!
Listen to François and Louise comparing different regions of France. Are these statements true or false? (*Answers on page 128.*)

	VRAI	FAUX
a) Louise adore la montagne.		
b) François préfère la Provence.		
c) Louise aime la mer.		
d) Louise et son mari ont une villa en Bourgogne.		

2   Lisez! Ecrivez!
Complete the gaps in these sentences with **plus** (more), **moins** (less) or **meilleur(s)** (better/best). (*Answers on page 128.*)

La Provence a le _____ climat de France.

C'est _____ calme en Provence qu'en Auvergne.
Les vins de Bourgogne sont _____ que les vins de Provence.
Sur la Côte d'Azur il fait _____ chaud qu'en Bretagne.

3 … et parlez français!
Refer to the **En français** section for this exercise. Your favourite French region
is Burgundy (**la Bourgogne**). Argue with Chantal, who prefers Brittany (**la
Bretagne**). Reply to each of Chantal's assertions, by saying **Oui, mais en
Bourgogne, etc.**' (*Answers on page 128.*)

1. … it is warmer.
2. … there are fewer tourists.
3. … the cuisine is better.
4. … the wines are cheaper.

En français

Comparatives
1. To say 'more/less than', you need:

plus que	more than	**moins que**	less than

e.g. **Lyon est plus grand que Grenoble** – 'Lyon is bigger than Grenoble'.
Notes: (i)   The French say 'more big', not 'bigger'.
       (ii)   **Que** is used to mean 'than'.

2. To say 'the most/least' you just put the definite article **le/la/les** in front of **plus**
('the most') or **moins** ('the least').

La plus/moins belle ville	The most/least beautiful town

If the adjective, e.g. **cher**, *follows* the noun, the definite article appears *twice*.

Les robes les plus/moins chères	The dearest/cheapest dresses

3. **plus/moins de** means 'more/less of' something.

plus/moins de touristes	more/fewer tourists

En France

The French for 'country' is **pays**, but when a Frenchman says **mon pays** he will
often be talking about his own region of France rather than about the whole
country, and it is as important to have some awareness of the regional differences
of France – climate, landscape, history, culture, traditions, cuisine – as it is to be
able to understand and speak the language. Try to memorize the names of the 22
regions in the map on page 79.

Language extra

These exercises provide extra practice in some of the important language skills you have learnt in Units 14–36. Check your answers on pages 128–9.

A. Object pronouns

Answer the questions, replacing the noun underlined with an object pronoun **le/la/l'/les** as in the example.

	e.g. Vous prenez <u>la robe</u>?	Oui, je la prends.
1.	Vous connaissez <u>Marie</u>?	Oui, je _____ .
2.	Vous aimez <u>ce vin</u>?	Oui, je _____ .
3.	Je quitte <u>l'autoroute</u>?	Oui, vous _____ .
4.	Vous avez visité <u>Paris</u>?	Oui, nous _____ .
5.	Tu connais <u>Anne et Marc</u>?	Oui, je _____ .

B. Past and future

Change these sentences from the present tense to a) the past and b) the future.

e.g. Je parle français
   a) J'ai parlé français   b) Je vais parler français

1. Je réserve la chambre.
   a) J' _____   b) Je _____

2. Il téléphone à Nice.
   a) Il _____   b) Il _____

3. Nous décidons.
   a) Nous _____   b) Nous _____

4. Je présente mon ami.
   a) J' _____   b) Je _____

5. Vous essayez le pantalon?
   a) Vous _____   b) Vous _____

C. Numbers and times (12-hour clock)

Can you say and write the following in French?

Numbers   70 71 79 82 90 99 100 150 570
Times   3 o'clock   5 past 4   Half past 6   A quarter to 10

D. En/au/aux

'In' or 'to' a country or French region is **en**, **au** or **aux**. Use the correct word for the following.

_____ France	_____ Espagne	_____ Portugal	_____ Suisse
_____ Angleterre	_____ Etats-Unis	_____ Canada	_____ Italie
_____ Normandie	_____ Allemagne	_____ Bretagne	_____ Provence

Testez-vous!

Test yourself to see how much you can remember from Units 14–36. Check your answers on the recording.

In French, how do you …

1. Say 'I would like an apple tart.'
2. Ask 'Is breakfast included?'
3. Say 'It's a bit expensive.'
4. Ask 'Can I reserve by phone?'
5. Say 'My credit card is valid till May 1998.'
6. Ask 'What time does the train arrive in Nice?'
7. Ask 'Is it necessary to change?'
8. Ask the assistant 'Can I see this watch?'
9. Say 'I like it a lot.'
10. Say 'I'll take it.'
11. Ask the bank cashier 'Can you change a 500 franc note?'
12. Say 'I hate snails.'
13. Say 'I would like to rent a car for one week.'
14. Say 'I was born in (your town).'
15. Introduce a friend to someone.
16. Wish someone 'Safe journey.'
17. Say 'I've no small change.'
18. Say 'I phoned last week.'
19. Spell your name.
20. Say 'The weather is bad.'
21. Ask 'What is the time?'
22. Say 'It is too small.'
23. Say 'I've a headache.'
24. Say 'I don't like fish.'
25. Say 'I've broken down.'

In the café

Paying for drinks and snacks

Vocabulaire

From now on nouns, adjectives, verbs etc. are grouped separately for ease of reference. Nouns are given with their gender and verbs appear in their infinitive form.

addition (f)	bill
crêpe (f)	crêpe, pancake
crevette (f)	prawn
croque-monsieur (m)	toasted cheese and ham sandwich
demi-litre (m)	half-litre
(vin) rouge (m)	red (wine)
glace (f)	ice-cream
limonade (f)	lemonade
prêt	ready
finir (**de**)	to finish
téléphoner (**à**)	to telephone
revenir (irreg)	to come back
j'arrive	I'm coming, right away
Qu'est-ce que vous avez pris?	What did you have?
sans problèmes	no problem
On y va?	Shall we go?

Dialogue

Françoise	Alors, les enfants, on a fini de manger? Florence, tu as bu ta limonade?
Jules	Françoise, tu veux payer? Moi, je vais téléphoner à l'hôtel. Mademoiselle, on peut avoir l'addition, s'il vous plaît?
Waitress	Oui, monsieur, j'arrive.
Jules	Est-ce qu'on peut téléphoner d'ici?
Waitress	Au sous-sol, monsieur. Madame, qu'est-ce que vous avez pris?
Françoise	Une crêpe aux crevettes, un croque-monsieur et un demi-litre de rouge. Puis deux glaces et une limonade.
Waitress	Alors 92F50. Merci, madame.
Françoise	Florence, Henri. Vous êtes prêts? Voilà papa qui revient.
Jules	Tu as payé, chérie? Bien. Alors j'ai téléphoné et j'ai réservé la chambre. Sans problèmes. On y va?

Exercices

1 Ecoutez!

Put a tick against each order that you hear mentioned. (*Answers on page 129.*)

red wine	___	white coffee	___	ham sandwich	___	cream cake	___
salami pizza	___	prawn pancake	___	draught beer	___	lemon tea	___
orange juice	___	ham pizza	___	black coffee	___	apple tart	___

2 Lisez! Ecrivez!

Use the perfect tense verb forms on the next page to complete this list of things which Jules might want to say he has done today. The first one is already written in. (*Answers on page 129.*)

téléphoné   **mangé**   **bu**   **réservé**   **fini**   **payé**

	mangé	un croque-monsieur
	_____	l'addition
	_____	ma bière
J'ai	_____	à l'hôtel
	_____	la chambre
	_____	de manger

3   ... et parlez français!

Now confirm that you have done various things as asked on the recording. (*Answers on page 129.*)

1. Say yes, you have paid the bill.
2. Say yes, you have telephoned the hotel.
3. Say yes, you have reserved the room.
4. Say yes, you have drunk your beer.

En français

1. *-IR verbs.* You are now familiar with **-ER** verbs in the present tense. There is another, much smaller, group of regular verbs to learn – those with the infinitive in **-IR**, e.g. **finir** – 'to finish', **choisir** – 'to choose'. Check the endings in the Verb Tables on page 131 and note the characteristic **-iss-** for the **nous**, **vous** and **ils/elles** forms of the present tense, e.g. **nous finissons**, **ils finissent**. (The final **-ent** is silent, as with **-ER** verbs.)

2. *The perfect tense.* You met examples of this tense, used for past events, in Units 10 and 27. Further examples occur in this unit.

j'ai téléphoné   j'ai réservé   tu as payé

For **j'ai** you can substitute **il/elle a**, **tu as**, **nous avons**, **vous avez**, **ils/elles ont**. Notice how this tense adapts to other persons in the dialogue.

tu as payé   on a fini   vous avez pris

3. In conversation **on** often replaces **nous**.

On a fini de manger?   Have we finished eating?

En France

An addition to the list of eating places in France should be **la crêperie**. Brittany (**la Bretagne**) is the true home of the **crêpe**, which comes with all kinds of filling, sweet and savoury. Perhaps the best known is the **crêpe Suzette**, flavoured with **Grand Marnier** or **cognac**.

At the hotel

Confirming a reservation

réservation (f)	reservation
homme (m)	man
registre (m)	register
nombre (m)	number (quantity)
impossible	impossible
étrange	strange
jeune	young
écossais	Scottish
comprendre (irreg)	to understand
vérifier	to check
encore	again
Comment?	What?
il y a deux semaines	two weeks ago
ne … aucun(e)	not … any
C'est bien vous/moi	It *is* you/me
Ce n'est pas grave	It's not serious, No harm done

Dialogue

Mr McTavish	J'ai une réservation au nom de McTavish.
Receptionist	Pardon? Comment ça s'écrit, monsieur?
Mr McTavish	Alors je l'épelle – M C T A V I S H.
Receptionist	Je suis désolée, je ne trouve aucune réservation à ce nom, monsieur.
Mr McTavish	Comment? Mais je ne comprends pas. C'est impossible. J'ai écrit il y a deux semaines et j'ai téléphoné pour confirmer.
Receptionist	C'est étrange. Vous dites que vous avez téléphoné?
Mr McTavish	Oui. J'ai parlé à un jeune homme…
Receptionist	Alors, ce n'est pas moi, monsieur! Attendez, je vais vérifier encore dans le registre. Ah, je l'ai trouvé. On a réservé une chambre à deux lits, pour trois nuits, au nom de 'M. Tavish'. C'est bien vous, monsieur? Vous êtes anglais?
Mr McTavish	C'est bien moi, mais je ne suis pas anglais. Je suis écossais.
Receptionist	Excusez-moi, monsieur.
Mr McTavish	Ce n'est pas grave.

Exercices

1 Ecoutez! Ecrivez!

A tourist is phoning to confirm her hotel reservation. Write in her details on the booking register below. (*Answers on page 129.*)

Hôtel de la Plage	
Nom, prénom	
Nationalité	
Nombre de personnes	
Numéro de chambre	
Date d'arrivée	
Date de départ	

2   Lisez! Ecrivez!

Test your memory – cover up the dialogue opposite and complete these
phrases. The last two words are missing in each line.

a) J'ai écrit il y a _____ _____.
b) Je n'ai aucune réservation à _____ _____.
c) Vous dites que vous _____ _____?
d) J'ai parlé à un _____ _____.
e) Je vais vérifier dans _____ _____.

3   … et parlez français!

Using the recording from Exercise 1, stop the tape as necessary to speak the
part of the tourist. Use the details you have written in the register in Exercise 1
as prompts. Check your answers on the recording.

En français

1.   Some more verbs in the *perfect tense*.
J'ai écrit – I wrote (or 'I have written'). Note the *irregular* past participle – **écrit**.
On a réservé – another example of **on** being used to mean 'we' or perhaps
'they'. It enables the receptionist to keep the responsibility for the booking error
vague, by saying '**On a réservé**' instead of '**j'ai réservé**' – *I* have reserved'.

2.   **Je ne trouve aucune réservation** – 'I can't find any reservation'. The negative
expression **ne … aucun** (feminine **aucune**) – 'not any' is placed round the verb like
ne … pas.

3.   A second meaning of **il y a** (Unit 6) is 'ago'. Notice the word order is different in
French – first **il y a**, then the length of time.

il y a deux semaines	two weeks ago

En France

There are many ways of saying sorry in French. **Excusez-moi!** or **Pardon!** to
attract someone's attention, but also for something wrong that you have done. **Je
m'excuse** is another way of apologising. For something unfortunate for which the
speaker is not to blame, for example a hotel receptionist saying the hotel is full:
Je regrette or **(Je suis) désolé(e), monsieur/madame** …

Numbers

Dates and seasons

Vocabulaire

recette (f)	recipe
grand-mère (f)	grandmother
propriétaire (m/f)	owner
cuisinier/ère (m/f)	cook
plongeur/euse (m/f)	washer-up
fête (f)	festival, public holiday
rentrée (f)	return to work/school
gîte (m)	(rented) farmhouse
délicieux (f -euse)	delicious
régional	regional
familial	family (adj)
imaginer	to imagine
un peu de tout	a bit of everything
il ne manque pas	there's no lack
pendant tout l'été	all through the summer

Dialogue

Waitress	Alors, cent cinquante francs. Merci, monsieur.
Yves	C'était délicieux. C'est un plat régional?
Waitress	Un peu, oui. Un peu familial aussi. La recette vient de ma grand-mère. Elle a 93 ans!
Annick	Ah oui? Et c'est vous, la propriétaire?
Waitress	Avec mon frère, oui. Depuis 78. Propriétaire, cuisinière, plongeuse, serveuse, un peu de tout!
Annick	Il y a beaucoup de travail en cette saison, j'imagine.
Waitress	En juillet et en août, oui. Surtout les jours de fête – le quatorze juillet et le quinze août, par exemple. Après la rentrée – en automne, en hiver, c'est plus calme. Mais au printemps et pendant tout l'été il ne manque pas de travail … Vous êtes en vacances?
Yves	Oui. Nous avons loué un gîte jusqu'au dix août.

Les quatre	**printemps** (m)	spring
saisons	**été** (m)	summer
The four	**automne** (m)	autumn
seasons	**hiver** (m)	winter

Exercices

1 Ecoutez!

Only six of the dates below are on your recording. Tick the boxes as you hear them. (*Answers on page 129.*)

3/v/98		17/vii/89		22/viii/47		1/ix/92	
31/xii/55		11/ii/97		16/i/61		21/iii/89	

2 Ecrivez!

The crossword below contains the names of the four seasons in French. Can you complete it by writing in the twelve months of the year? (*Answers on page 129.*)

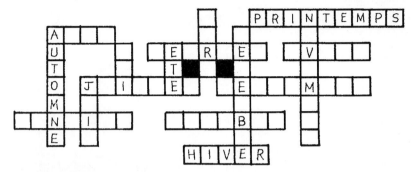

3 ... et parlez français!

Read aloud the dates ticked in the boxes in Exercise 1. Check your answers on the recording.

En français

1. *Possessive adjectives.* **Mon** and **ma** are used again in the dialogue. Here is the complete table of possessive adjectives.

	Masc.	Fem.	Plural		Masc/Fem.	Plural
my	mon	ma	mes	our	notre	nos
your (fam.)	ton	ta	tes	your (formal)	votre	vos
his/her	son	sa	ses	their	leur	leurs

2. 'In' for months, seasons and years is **en**.

En juin	*In* June	**En hiver**	*In* winter	**En 78**	In '78

There is one exception: **Au printemps** – '*In* spring'.

3. Note all French days, months and seasons are masculine and all begin with a small letter.

En France

The French do not have 'bank holidays', but in addition to **Noël** (Christmas), **le Jour de l'An** (New Year's Day), **Pâques** (Easter) and **la Pentecôte** (Whitsun), note the following: **la Fête du Travail** (Labour Day, 1st May), **le huit mai** (commemorating the end of World War 2), **la Fête Nationale** (Bastille Day, 14th July), **l'Assomption** (Assumption, 15th August), **la Toussaint** (All Saints Day, 1st November), and **le Jour de l'Armistice** (11th November, World Wars 1 and 2).

Talking about yourself

Describing people

Vocabulaire

cheveux (m.pl)	hair
blue-jean (m)	jeans
chemise (f)	shirt
costume (m)	suit
cravate (f)	tie
lunettes (f.pl)	glasses
verres de contact (m.pl)	contact lenses
grand	big, tall
petit	small, short
cadet/cadette (m/f)	younger
mince	slim
long	long
court	short
brun	brown
gris	grey
blond	blond, fair
habillé	dressed
sympathique	likeable, friendly
sérieux (f -euse)	serious
élégant	elegant
porter	to wear, to carry
Comment est-il?	What's he like?

Dialogue

Julie	Parlez-moi de votre famille, Vincent. Vous avez des frères ou des sœurs?
Vincent	J'ai une sœur cadette et un frère aîné. Ma sœur s'appelle Véronique. Elle a 29 ans. Elle est très jolie, très sympathique. Elle a les cheveux longs, les yeux bruns et elle est habillée toujours en blue-jean et en chemise d'homme.
Julie	Et votre frère, comment est-il?
Vincent	Jean-Paul a trente-quatre ans. Très sérieux, très élégant, il porte des cravates et des costumes gris. Il est assez grand et mince. Il a les cheveux blonds très courts et les yeux bleus.
Julie	Il porte des lunettes, comme vous?
Vincent	Non, il porte des verres de contact.

Exercices

1 Ecoutez!

Refer to the **En France** section, then listen to these descriptions of Anne and Marc and circle the words which apply. (*Answers on page 129.*)

Anne is *tall/short*, has *long/short* hair, wears *glasses/contact lenses*, dresses *formally/casually* and is very *active/lazy*.

Marc has *long/short* hair, dresses *formally/casually*, wears *glasses/contact lenses* and is *older/younger* than Anne.

2   Lisez! Ecrivez!
Use the words below to complete the sentences. (*Answers on page 129.*)

**lunettes   cheveux blonds   cravate noire   grand   costume élégant
chemise bleue   yeux bleus   mince**

Pierre est _____ et _____, et porte des _____.
Lucie a les _____ _____ et les _____ _____.
Henri porte un _____ _____, une _____
_____ et une _____ _____.

3   ... et parlez français!
Use the correct information in Exercise 1 and speak aloud the descriptions of
Anne and Marc. Check your answers on the recording.

En français

1. When describing parts of the body use **le/la/les**.

Il a <u>les</u> cheveux longs	He has long hair

When referring to clothing/accessories use **un(e)** or **du/de la/des**.

Il porte <u>des</u> lunettes	He wears glasses

2. Note the verb **porter** means both 'to wear' and 'to carry'.

Elle porte une robe	She's wearing a dress
Elle porte un paquet	She's carrying a parcel

It will normally be clear from the context which meaning is intended.

3. The adjectives **petit** (small) and **grand** (big), mean 'short' and 'tall' respectively
when used to describe people.

En France

Paris is of course the traditional home of fashion, but even this preserve of
French culture has been invaded by '**franglais**' and the vocabulary of fashion and
clothing is today rife with borrowings from English such as **le blue-jean**, **le short**,
le pull-over, **le jogging**, **le tee-shirt** and so on. Some, however, are 'false
friends', e.g. **les baskets** are 'trainers'.

Out and about

Finding a place to park

Vocabulaire

parcmètre (m)	parking meter
seconde (f)	second
sens unique (m)	one-way street
pièce (f)	coin
défense de stationner	no parking
voie barrée	road blocked, closed off
passage interdit	no entry
partout	everywhere
de l'autre côté	on the other side
trop tard	too late
sauf vélos (m)	except cycles
C'est permis (de)	Is it allowed (to)
faire demi-tour	to do a U-turn
C'est pas vrai!	I don't believe it (lit. It's not true)
Zut!	Damn! Blast!
Allez, circulez!	Go on, keep moving!
Pardon, monsieur l'agent	Excuse me, officer
Quelle chance!	What luck!

Dialogue

Anne   Oh, c'est pas vrai! Partout 'Défense de stationner'.
Muriel   Anne! De l'autre côté, tu vois? Il y a une place. Vite!
Anne   Zut! Trop tard!
Agent   Allez, circulez!
Anne   Pardon, monsieur l'agent! C'est permis de stationner ici une seconde?
Agent   Non, madame! Il y a un parking rue Verlaine, derrière l'église.
Anne   Je peux faire demi-tour?
Agent   Mais non, c'est sens unique! Vous allez tout droit et vous prenez la troisième rue à droite.
Anne   Merci! Alors Muriel. Première ... 'Voie barrée' ... Deuxième ... 'Passage interdit à tous véhicules sauf vélos.' Oh, regarde, Muriel. Quelle chance – un parcmètre! Et c'est libre! Tu as des pièces?

Exercices

1   **Ecoutez!**
On your recording a policeman is giving motorists a series of instructions. Can you match each to the English versions below? Write nos 1 to 6 in the boxes. (*Answers on page 129.*)

☐ Park across the street.
☐ Drive straight on.
☐ Keep moving!

☐ No U-turns.
☐ Free meter available.
☐ No parking here.

2 Lisez!

Which traffic signs go with which captions? (Refer first to the **En France** section on this page.) (*Answers on page 129.*)

i) ii) iii) iv) v)

| a)
ATTENTION
ENFANTS | b)
ZONE
D'ENLEVEMENT | c)
DEFENSE DE
TOURNER A GAUCHE | d)
ZONE
PIETONNE | e)
PARKING
SAUF AUTOCARS |

3 ... et parlez français!

You are looking for a place to park. Stop a policeman and ask for help. Start by saying **Pardon, monsieur l'agent**. Then use the prompts below to ask three questions. (*Answers on page 129.*)

1. Is there a car park near here?
2. Is it far?
3. Can I do a U-turn?

En français

1. **Il y a un parking rue Verlaine**. Note 'in' or 'on' is not translated before the name of a street or square.

2. **Regarde!** is the **tu** equivalent of the **vous** form **Regardez!** (Units 11 and 22). To form the imperative of an **-ER** verb, drop the **-s** from the present tense.

| **Tu regard<u>es</u>** You look | **Regarde!** Look! |

(In any case this is not a problem when speaking, since the final **-s** is normally silent.)

3. In everyday speech the French frequently omit the **ne** from negative expressions, e.g. **C'est pas vrai!** for **Ce n'est pas vrai!**

En France

As well as the **parcmètre** (or **parcomètre**), increasing use is made of the **horodateur** (pay-and-display machine). In a **zone bleue** you will need a **disque de stationnement**, 'parking disc', obtainable at roadside kiosks and petrol stations. **Zone piétonne** means pedestrian precinct, whilst if you park in a **zone d'enlèvement** you may get back to find your vehicle has been **enlevé** – 'removed'! – in which case, don't forget to address the nearest **agent de police** (policeman) politely – as **monsieur l'agent!**

Public transport

Conversation on the train

Vocabulaire

place (f)	place
valise (f)	suitcase
Camembert (m)	Camembert – soft cheese
wagon-restaurant (m)	dining car
panier (m)	basket
charmant	charming
aimable	kind
ouvert	open
fermé	closed
visiter	to visit (places)
vendre	to sell
Prenez-en	Have some

Dialogue

Mme Berry	Cette place est libre, monsieur?
M. Sagan	Oui, oui. Attendez, madame. Je peux vous aider avec la valise?
Mme Berry	Merci beaucoup, monsieur. Vous êtes très gentil.
M. Sagan	Vous allez loin, madame?
Mme Berry	Je descends à Besançon. Je vais voir mon fils et sa famille. Vous connaissez Besançon, monsieur?
M. Sagan	Un peu. Je l'ai visité l'année dernière. C'est une ville charmante. Vous êtes de Besançon, madame?
Mme Berry	Non, je suis née à Nantes, monsieur.
Inspector	Messieurs-dames! Vos billets, s'il vous plaît. Merci.
M. Sagan	Le wagon-restaurant est ouvert?
Inspector	C'est fermé, monsieur. Il y a un bar où on vend des sandwichs. Merci madame, monsieur.
Mme Berry	Monsieur, j'ai du pâté et du Camembert dans mon panier. Prenez-en, monsieur. Et de la baguette. J'en ai fait beaucoup trop pour une seule personne.
M. Sagan	Vous êtes trop aimable, madame. Mais j'accepte très volontiers!

Exercices

1 Ecoutez!

Test your understanding by saying whether the statements are true or false. (*Answers on page 129.*)

a) The man is going to Avignon.
b) The woman is visiting her friend.
c) Her friend lives in Paris.
d) The man was born in Paris.

VRAI	FAUX

2 Lisez! Ecrivez!

Write in the missing verbs in the sentences opposite from the dialogue between Mme Berry and M. Sagan.

a) Je _____ vous aider?
b) Vous _____ loin?
c) Vous _____ Besançon?
d) Vous _____ trop aimable.
e) J' _____ très volontiers.
f) Il y a un bar où on _____ des sandwichs.

En français

1.   **-RE verbs** are the third and final group of regular verbs to be learnt. **Vendre** is an example. It follows the pattern for the present tense in the Verb Tables on page 131.

Je vends, tu vends, il/elle vend, etc.

The **je**, **tu** and **il/elle** forms are all pronounced the same. In the perfect tense **-RE** verbs end in **-u**.

J'ai vendu   I (have) sold

2.   Did you notice the verbs in the *perfect tense* in the dialogue? **J'ai visité** and **J'ai fait** are both preceded by *object pronouns* to say 'it' and 'of it'.

Je l'ai visité	I visited <u>it</u>
J'en ai fait beaucoup trop	I made much too much <u>of it</u>

Use **le/la** (**l'** before a vowel or silent **h**) for 'him', 'her' and 'it', and **les** to say 'them'. **En** can mean 'of it', 'of them'.

3.   Note that when you are *telling* someone to do something (the imperative) object pronouns like **le** and **en** *follow* the verb.

Prenez-le!	Take it!	**Prenez-en!**	Take some (of it)!

4.   Note **Je vais voir mon fils** in the dialogue – 'I'm going to see (i.e. visit) my son'. Keep the verb **visiter** for visiting places, not people.

En France

Every French region has an adjective to describe its inhabitants. The same applies to towns and cities. You will be familiar with **parisien(ne)**, but you will also commonly hear people from Lyon, Bordeaux, Grenoble or Marseille proudly declare themselves to be **lyonnais(e)**, **bordelais(e)**, **grenoblois(e)**, and **marseillais(e)**. **La Marseillaise** is also of course France's national anthem.

Shopping

At the delicatessen

Vocabulaire

morceau (m)	piece
tête de veau (f)	brawn (lit. head of veal/calf)
pâté de campagne (m)	coarse 'country' pâté
gruyère (m)	Swiss gruyère cheese
saucisson à l'ail (m)	garlic sausage
salade de riz (f)	rice salad
cru	raw
noir	black
pimenté	hot, spicy
enlever	to take away
goûter	to taste
C'est un peu plus	It's a bit over
en promotion	on introductory offer
Autre chose?	Anything else?
Ça va comme ça	That's all

Dialogues

1.

Assistant	Vous désirez, madame?
Customer	200 grammes de tête de veau, s'il vous plaît.
Assistant	C'est un peu plus. 250 grammes. J'enlève une tranche?
Customer	Non, ça va. Et le saucisson à l'ail? Celui-là, au fond.
Assistant	Celui-ci? C'est en promotion, madame. 24F40 le kilo.
Customer	Alors, un demi-kilo.
Assistant	Voilà. Avec ça, madame?
Customer	200 grammes de pâté de campagne, 300 grammes de salade de riz et un morceau de gruyère.
Assistant	Autre chose, madame?
Customer	Ça va comme ça. Merci.

2.

Customer	Je voudrais des olives.
Assistant	Celles-ci? Les noires?
Customer	Non, les vertes, elles sont pimentées?
Assistant	Oui, madame. Vous voulez goûter?
Customer	Mmm! Délicieuses!
Assistant	Combien vous en voulez?
Customer	Euh, 150 grammes, s'il vous plaît.

Exercices

1   Ecoutez!
Listen to shoppers A and B in the **charcuterie** (delicatessen).
Indicate in the boxes what is bought and how much. (*Answers on page 129.*)

	Grams (Write	Slices the	Pieces quantity)	Ham (Tick	Cheese or	Salami leave	Olives blank)
A							
B							

2   Lisez!
Match these questions with their answers. (*Answers on page 129.*)

a) Elles sont pimentées?
b) Celles-ci? Les noires?
c) Combien vous en voulez?
d) J'enlève une tranche?
e) Vous voulez goûter?

i)   150 grammes, s'il vous plaît.
ii) Merci. Mmm! Délicieuses.
iii) Oui, madame.
iv) Non, les vertes.
v)   Non, ça va.

3   ... et parlez français!
Now re-create the dialogue at the **charcuterie**. (*Answers on page 129.*)

1. Start by asking for a piece of gruyère.
2. 300 grammes.
3. You'd also like some black olives.
4. 150.
5. And you'd like some rice salad.
6. 200 grammes.
7. Finally, you ask for some brawn (head of veal).
8. 3 slices.
9. That's all.

En français

In the last unit you met the pronoun **en**. You will frequently hear it used, with the meaning 'of it', 'of them', 'some of it/them', usually coming before the verb.
Combien vous en voulez? How much (of it/them) do you want? Try using it yourself when you are asked how many of something you have got, children, for example.

Combien d'enfants avez-vous?   How many children do you have?
J'en ai deux.   I've got two (of them).

(Note, if you use **en** you do *not* repeat **enfants**.)

En France

The French **charcuterie** is justly famous for the quality and variety of its dairy produce, cold meats and sausages – **jambon**, **salami**, **saucisson** (not to be confused with **saucisse**, usually for frying or grilling, like the delicious, spicy **merguez** from North Africa) or, if you are partial to brawn, **tête de veau**. Cold meats are **fumé** (smoked) or **cru** (unsmoked, lit. 'raw'). Prices will be **le kilo** or **la pièce** for individual items such as cold **artichauts farcis** (stuffed artichokes).

Finally, France traditionally boasts over 400 varieties of **fromage,** giving rise to President de Gaulle's famous despairing remark: How can anyone hope to govern a country which has 400 different kinds of cheese!

Services

At the bank

Vocabulaire

dollar (m)	dollar
livre (f)	pound
cours (m)	exchange rate
commission (f)	commission
signature (f)	signature
chiffre (m)	figure
lettre (f)	letter
somme (f)	amount
Eurochèque (m)	Eurocheque
moins	less, minus
passer	to pass, to go over
Puis-je?	May I? Can I?
retirer	to withdraw
encaisser	to cash
écrire (irreg)	to write
vous l'écrivez	you write it

Dialogues

Tourist	Bonjour. Je voudrais changer de l'argent.
Clerk	Qu'est-ce que vous avez? Des dollars? Des livres?
Tourist	J'ai cent livres sterling. Quel est le cours de la livre aujourd'hui?
Clerk	Attendez, monsieur. C'est 7F50. Alors, 750F moins notre commission. Passez à la caisse, s'il vous plaît, monsieur.
Tourist	Puis-je retirer de l'argent avec ma carte Visa?
Clerk	Donnez-moi votre carte et votre passeport, s'il vous plaît. Et votre signature ici ... Oui, merci monsieur.
Tourist	Je peux encaisser un Eurochèque ici?
Clerk	Oui, madame. Vous avez votre carte et votre passeport? Merci. Signez le chèque ici.
Tourist	Et j'écris la somme ici? En chiffres, oui?
Clerk	Oui, et vous l'écrivez en lettres ici, madame. Voilà. A la caisse numéro un, s'il vous plaît.

Exercices

1 Ecoutez!

Listen to this conversation at the bank counter and circle the correct phrase in italics from each of the sentences below. (*Answers on page 129.*)

The customer wants to *cash a Eurocheque/change £100*.
The date is *Aug 3/Aug 13*.
She writes the amount in *figures/letters*.
The rate for the pound is *7F40/7F30*.
She is told to go to cashier's counter *No. 2/No. 3*.

2 Lisez! Ecrivez!

Insert one of the following verbs in each of the spaces below. (*Answers on page 129.*)

retirer   écrivez   encaisser   passez   changer   donnez

a) Puis-je _____ de l'argent?
b) _____ la date ici, s'il vous plaît.
c) _____ à la caisse, madame.
d) Je voudrais _____ un Eurochèque.
e) _____ - moi votre passeport, s'il vous plaît.
f) Est-ce que je peux _____ de l'argent avec ma Mastercard?

3 ... et parlez français!

Now go to the bank and change some money. You start the conversation. Use the prompts below. (*Answers on page 129.*)

1. Tell the cashier you would like to change some money.
2. Say that you have £150.
3. Find out the rate for the pound.
4. And the commission. How much is it?

En français

1. The verb **écrire** is **irregular**. (See Verb Tables, pages 131–2.)

J'écris	I write	**Vous écrivez**	You write

Listen to this verb on your recording after Exercise 3.

2. Note the alternative way of asking 'May I?' 'Can I?' – either **Je peux?** or **Puis-je?**

En France

Obtaining cash in France presents few problems – opening hours apart (Unit 18) – either with your **carte de crédit** or your **chèques de voyage** (traveller's cheques), often called simply **les travellers**. Banknotes (**billets**) come in denominations of 20, 50, 100, 200 and 500 francs. There are coins (**pièces**) for 1, 2, 5 and 10 francs, and 5, 10, 20 and 50 **centimes**.

Outside normal banking hours you can change your money at the **Bureau de Change**, in large hotels or at one of the cash dispensers (**distributeurs**) outside the high street banks.

Eating out

Cheeses and desserts

Vocabulaire

dessert (m)	dessert
plateau (m)	tray
mousse au chocolat (f)	chocolate mousse
tarte aux abricots (f)	apricot tart
glace aux fraises (f)	strawberry ice cream
chèvre (f)	goat
digestif (m)	(after-dinner) liqueur
adorer	to adore
vouloir (irreg)	to want
prendre (irreg)	to take
Que prenez-vous?	What will you have?
je prendrai bien	I *will* have
Qu'est-ce que tu as?	What have you got?
donne-moi	give me
Veux-tu?	Will you?
moi non plus	me neither

Dialogue

Waitress	Que prenez-vous comme dessert?
Henri	Oh, moi, je ne prends pas de dessert. Apportez-moi le plateau de fromages, s'il vous plaît.
Sophie	Moi, je prendrai bien un dessert.
Waitress	Alors, mousse au chocolat, tarte aux abricots, glace aux fraises.
Antoine	J'adore la glace aux fraises. Et une demi-bouteille de Vouvray....
Sophie	... Tu veux un peu de fromage, Antoine?
Antoine	Oui, qu'est-ce que tu as là comme fromages? Du Brie, du Camembert, du St Paulin, du Boursin ... et ça, c'est du fromage de chèvre? Alors, donne-moi un petit morceau, veux-tu? J'adore le fromage de chèvre...
Waitress	... Messieurs-dames? Un café? Un digestif?
Antoine	Non, je ne veux pas de café, merci.
Sophie	Moi non plus.
Antoine	Juste l'addition, s'il vous plaît.
Waitress	Oui, tout de suite, monsieur.

Exercices

1 Ecoutez!

Play the part of the waiter and take down the orders as you hear them. Don't worry too much about the spelling – you can check them later in the vocabulary. (*Answers on page 129.*)

2   Lisez! Ecrivez!

Compose your own restaurant menu. Arrange the dishes below under the headings in the menu alongside. (*Answers on page 129.*)

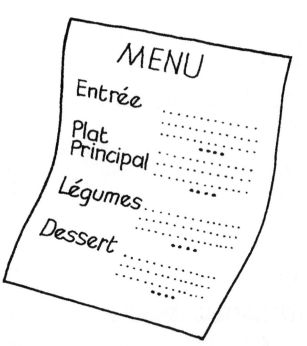

Haricots verts
Glace aux fraises
Filet de sole
Fruits de mer
Petits pois
Mousse au chocolat
Poulet rôti
Soupe à l'oignon
Tarte aux abricots
Choucroute garnie
Pommes frites
Moules marinière

3   … et parlez français!

Order a meal for yourself and two companions from the menu above. Use the prompts below. (*Answers on page 129.*)

1. Order one mussels and two seafoods.
2. One roast chicken, one steak with chips and one fillet of sole.
3. Green beans and peas.
4. One chocolate mousse, one strawberry ice-cream and one apricot tart.

En français

1. *Negatives*. Two more verbs with **ne … pas** in this dialogue. As well as **ne … pas** you have met **ne … aucun** (Unit 39). You should also learn **ne … plus** – 'no more', **ne … jamais** – 'never', **ne … rien** – 'nothing' and **ne … personne** – 'no one'.

Je **n'**habite **plus** à Paris	I don't live in Paris any more
Je **ne** prends **jamais** de dessert	I never have any dessert
Je **ne** veux **rien**	I don't want anything
Je **ne** connais **personne**	I don't know anyone

2. Remember the irregular verb **AVOIR** –'to have' (Unit 6). **Tu as** is the informal equivalent of **vous avez** – 'you have', and is of course the form which is used between husband and wife.

En France

After coffee and a **digestif**, the bill. Bear in mind that, although in cafés and restaurants the word for 'bill' is **l'addition**, your hotel bill is **la note**, while elsewhere the normal word for a bill or an invoice is **la facture**.

Travel by car

At the petrol station

Vocabulaire

capot (m)	bonnet
pneu (m)	tyre
fermé à clé	locked
beaucoup plus rapide	much quicker
avancer	to move forward
ouvrir (irreg)	to open
remercier	to thank
à côté de	next to
De rien	Don't mention it
Bonne route!	Safe journey!

Dialogue

Attendant	Gas-oil?
Motorist	Oui. Faites le plein, s'il vous plaît.
Attendant	Avancez un peu ... Donnez-moi la clé, s'il vous plaît.
Motorist	Comment?
Attendant	La clé! – c'est fermé à clé.
Motorist	Oh, Pardon. Voilà.
Attendant	Alors, 82F30. Merci.
Motorist	Pouvez-vous vérifier l'huile? Et l'eau aussi?
Attendant	Ouvrez le capot, mademoiselle ... Et voilà, oui, ça va.
Motorist	Où est-ce que je peux vérifier mes pneus?
Attendant	Là-bas, à côté du restaurant.
Motorist	Merci. Euh, pour aller à Besançon, je prends la N83 ou l'autoroute?
Attendant	Prenez l'A36, mademoiselle. C'est moins intéressant mais c'est beaucoup plus rapide.
Motorist	Je vous remercie, monsieur.
Attendant	De rien, mademoiselle. Bonne route!

Exercices

1   Ecoutez!

Listen to another conversation at the petrol pumps and answer these questions. (*Answers on page 129.*)

a) Does the motorist want .... diesel ___? lead-free petrol ___?
b) Does the fuel cost .... 82F40 ___? 92F40 ___?
c) Does the attendant check the .... oil ___? water ___? tyres ___?
d) Is the motorist told to take the motorway ___? major road ___?

2   Lisez! Ecrivez!

Take one word from each column to make five instructions which you might hear at the petrol station. (*Answers on page 129.*)

Avancez	un	capot
Faites	le	autoroute
Ouvrez	l'	clé
Donnez-moi	le	peu
Prenez	la	plein

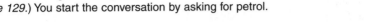

i _____ !   ii _____ !

iii _____ !   iv _____!

v _____!

3   ... et parlez français!

Re-create the dialogue in the petrol station using the prompts below. (*Answers on page 129.*) You start the conversation by asking for petrol.

1. Tell the attendant to fill up, 4-star lead-free, please.
2. Hand him the key and ask him if he can check the oil.
3. Say 'To go to Calais, do I take the motorway or the N43?'
4. Thank him and say goodbye.

En français

1.   To say 'What?' – **Comment?** is less polite than **Pardon?** though more polite than **Quoi?** which you will also hear.

2.   As a change from saying **Merci** try **Je vous remercie** – literally 'I thank you'. For 'Don't mention it' you will hear **De rien** as well as **Je vous en prie** (Unit 7).

3.   Learn the forms of the irregular verbs **faire** and **pouvoir** which both occur again in the dialogue to this unit. The forms of the verb **pouvoir** are on your recording after Exercise 3, and they both appear in the Verb Tables on pages 131–2.

4.   **Beaucoup** means 'a lot', 'much' or 'many'. Like other expressions of quantity (Unit 8), it is commonly used with **de** (or **d'**) and a following noun, e.g. **beaucoup d'argent** – 'a lot of money'; **beaucoup de touristes** – 'many tourists'.

En France

Speed limits in kilometres (8 kilometres = 5 miles) per hour are as follows (figures in brackets are for wet conditions):

Normal roads	50 in built-up areas, 90 (80) out of town
Dual carriageways	110 (90)
Motorways	130 (110)

There is a *minimum* speed of 80 km per hour for the outside lane of a motorway in good visibility.

Talking about France

National character

Dialogue

Jane On dit que les Anglais sont réservés, les Américains sont énergiques, les Allemands et les Japonais sont travailleurs, les Espagnols et les Italiens sont extravagants. Comment est le Français typique?

Olivier Le Français typique? Il est très individualiste, très romantique, assez indiscipliné … Qu'en penses-tu, Eve?

Eve Les Français? Quelquefois je les trouve un peu difficiles à connaître, si on n'est pas français.

Jane Oui, mais il faut faire un petit effort quand même. Tout d'abord, il faut parler la langue, n'est-ce pas?

Olivier Oui, c'est vrai. Nous sommes extrêmement fiers de notre culture, et de notre langue, bien sûr.

Jane C'est normal! Quant à moi, j'adore la langue française et le peuple français. Vive la France!

Exercices

1 Ecoutez!
Listen to another conversation. According to these speakers,
which of the following assertions are true? (*Answers on page 129.*)

	VRAI	FAUX
a) The French are sometimes difficult to know.		
b) The Italians are energetic.		
c) The Spanish are proud of their language.		
d) The Americans are hard-working.		
e) The English are disciplined.		

2 Lisez! Ecrivez!
Make up sentences using one word from each column. This exercise is just for
the practice – there is no 'right' or 'wrong' combination of words! But remember
the plural forms of the adjectives must end in **-s**.

e.g. Les Allemands sont très énergiques.

Italien		énergique
Américain	assez	réservé
Allemand	un peu	individualiste
Français	extrêmement	difficile à connaître
Anglais	très	extravagant
Espagnol		indiscipliné

En français

Notice the plural adjectives ending in **-s** in the dialogue. This does not change the
way they are pronounced. But remember when an **-e** is added for the *feminine* form
of the adjective, the preceding consonant *is* pronounced.

| the French people | **le peuple français** | (**s** *not* pronounced) |
| the French language | **la langue française** | (**s** pronounced) |

En France

The opinions expressed by the speakers in the dialogue to this unit are of course
controversial! It could certainly be argued that today's typical Frenchman is as
travailleur and **énergique** as he is **individualiste** and **indiscipliné**, while for
further evidence of that French pride and patriotic fervour expressed by **Vive la
France!** listen out for the sporting equivalent on the football or rugby pitch – **Allez
la France!** ('Come on France!')

 **Greetings and introductions**

New acquaintances

Vocabulaire

mairie (f)	town hall
citadelle (f)	citadel
librairie (f)	bookshop
livre (m)	book
beaux-arts (m)	fine arts
question (f)	question
histoire (f)	history
matinée (f)	morning
père (m)	father
passer	to pass, spend (time)
dîner	to dine
mieux que	better than
si	if
nous sommes montés	we went up
chez nous	at our place
chez l'antiquaire	at the antique dealer's
toute la matinée	all morning (long)
elle sera ravie	she will be delighted

 ### Dialogue

Mme Duval	Madame Leighton, je vous présente Monsieur Busard.
M. Busard	Enchanté de faire votre connaissance, madame.
Mrs Leighton	Enchantée, monsieur.
Mme Duval	Marc travaille à la mairie. Il connaît Besançon beaucoup mieux que nous. Si vous avez des questions sur l'histoire de la ville…
M. Busard	Vous avez déjà visité la vieille ville, madame?
Mrs Leighton	Nous sommes montés à la citadelle ce matin, puis nous avons vu le vieux quartier. Mon mari a acheté une très belle montre chez un antiquaire et notre fille a trouvé une librairie où elle a passé toute la matinée! Christine adore les vieux livres.
M. Busard	Ecoutez, madame. Venez dîner chez nous demain soir avec Jeanne et Henri. Mon père parle assez bien l'anglais, il sera ravi de vous connaître!

Exercices

 1 Ecoutez!

True or false? Listen to Julie talking about how she and her family spent their week in Besançon and tick the appropriate box. (*Answers on page 129.*)

	VRAI	FAUX
a) Julie bought a skirt in the market on Friday.		
b) Her father spent all day Tuesday in a café.		
c) On Wednesday her parents visited a museum.		
d) Julie and her brother went to a discotheque on Friday.		
e) Julie and Philippe went to the cinema with their parents on Saturday.		

2 Lisez! Ecrivez!

Choose one word from each column and make up four sentences.

e.g. Mercredi Pierre a visité la citadelle.

Lundi	Pierre	ai	visité	une belle montre
Mardi	nous	avez	trouvé	une librairie
Jeudi	vous	a	vu	un bon film
Hier	J'	avons	acheté	la citadelle

a) Lundi _____

b) Mardi _____

c) Jeudi _____

d) Hier _____

Note: there are no set answers to this exercise.

3 ... et parlez français!

Listen to the dialogue again. Stop the recording for Monsieur Busard and speak his part. Check your answers on the recording.

1. You are introduced to Mrs Leighton. Say 'Pleased to make your acquaintance.'
2. Mme Duval suggests you might be of help to Mrs Leighton. Ask her if she has already visited the old town.
3. When she has finished speaking, say 'Listen, come to dinner at my house this evening with Jeanne and Henri.' Add 'My father speaks English quite well. He'll be delighted to know you.'

En français

1. To use an adjective with a feminine noun you need simply add an **-e** in most cases (Unit 48). But note these two exceptions.

un beau bracelet	(masc.)	**une belle montre**	(fem.)
le vieux quartier	(masc.)	**la vieille ville**	(fem.)

Note that the **-ll-** is silent in **vieille**, but not in **ville**.

2. There are two French words meaning 'better/best'. The adjective **meilleur** agrees with the noun in the usual way: <u>la meilleure</u> cuisine – 'the best cooking'. The adverb **mieux** is invariable; it says something is *done* better: **Il connaît Paris mieux que moi** – 'He knows Paris better than me'.

En France

Few towns of any size in France do not boast, if not a **citadelle**, as in Besançon, at least an impressive **vieille ville**, or **vieux quartier**, full of shops with **meubles anciens** (antique furniture) and other **antiquités** (antiques), **galeries d'art** (art galleries) and **librairies** (bookshops – a library is **une bibliothèque**).

UNIT 50 In the café

More about telephoning

Vocabulaire	
appel (m)	call
tonalité (f)	tone
indicatif (m)	code
international	international
décrocher	to lift the receiver
mettre (irreg)	to put
composer	to dial
pas de problème	no problem
Je vais vous expliquer	I'll explain to you
C'est de la part de qui?	Who's calling?
Ne quittez pas	Hold on (lit. Don't go away)
C'est lui-même (fem. **elle-même**)	Speaking (lit. It's him/herself)
Comment allez-vous?	How are you?

Dialogues

1.	**Customer**	Puis-je téléphoner d'ici? C'est pour un appel international.
	Waiter	Pas de problème, madame. Vous téléphonez où? Quel pays?
	Customer	L'Angleterre.
	Waiter	Venez, madame. Je vais vous expliquer. Alors, vous décrochez, vous mettez vos pièces, vous composez le 00. Puis vous attendez la tonalité et vous composez le 44, c'est l'indicatif pour l'Angleterre, Ensuite, l'indicatif de la ville et le numéro.
2.	**Anne Pérez**	Allô! Je voudrais parler à M. Cléry, s'il vous plaît.
	Operator	C'est de la part de qui?
	Anne Pérez	Anne Pérez.
	Operator	Un instant, madame. Ne quittez pas …
	Anne Pérez	… Monsieur Cléry?
	M. Cléry	C'est lui-même.
	Anne Pérez	Bonjour, Monsieur Cléry. Je suis Anne Pérez!
	M. Cléry	Madame Pérez! Bonjour! Comment allez-vous?

Exercices

1 Ecoutez!
Listen to the dialogues again and tick the correct answers. (*Answers on page 129.*)

a) The French for 'coins' is **pays** ____ ? **pièces** ____ ?

b) After lifting the receiver the caller dials 00 ____ ? 44 ____ ?

c) **L'indicatif** means 'tone' ____ ? 'code' ____ ?

d) **Ne quittez pas** means 'Hold on' ____ ? 'Try again later' ____ ?

e) When a caller gets through, s/he says **Bonjour!** ____ **Allô** ____ ?

f) 'How are you?' is **Comment allez-vous**? ____ ? **C'est de la part de qui?** ____ ?

2 Lisez! Ecrivez!

Write in the missing instructions ending in **-ez**. The first is done for you.
(*Answers on page 129.*)

Alors, vous *décrochez*.
Vous _____vos pièces.
Vous _____ le 19.
Vous _____ la tonalité.
Ne _____ pas!

3 ... et parlez français!

Without looking at the dialogue opposite, re-create dialogue 2, using the
prompts below. You are telephoning Monsieur Cléry who works at the Paris
office of the company **PALIME SA** – 'PALIME Ltd'. (*Answers on page 129.*)
1. Say 'Hello! I would like to speak to Mr Clery, please.'
2. Say who you are.
3. Greet Monsieur Cléry. Say who you are and ask him how he is.

En français

1. **Mettre** – 'to put'. Refer to Verb Tables, page 132 and listen to the present tense
of this common irregular verb on your recording after Exercise 3.

2. You will remember that on being introduced to someone you say **Enchanté(e)!**
For subsequent meetings, the French for 'How are you?' is **Comment allez-vous?**
This is quite formal and should be used until you know the person well enough to
say **Comment ça va?** or just **Ça va?** The usual response is **Très bien, merci** –
'(I'm) very well, thank you.'

3. **Va** and **allez** are forms of the irregular verb **aller** (Unit 26).

En France

The nearest café is likely to be the
easiest place from which to make a
telephone call in France. The public
telephone box – **la cabine télé-
phonique** – is more difficult to find. In
some cafés you may need to buy a
telephone token – **un jeton** – at the
counter. Otherwise, and for calls
abroad, use coins or a **télécarte**. If
you need to speak to the operator,
dial **12** and, should you have run out
of money, ask for your call to be **en
PCV** (reverse charges), **s'il vous
plaît**. Finally, should you need an
emergency service, the number to
dial is **17**.

UNIT 51 At the hotel

Making a complaint

télévision (f)	television
téléviseur (m)	television (set)
ascenseur (m)	lift
quelqu'un	someone
marcher	to work (of equipment)
patienter	to be patient, to wait
toujours en panne	still out of order
Ah bon?	I see
jusqu'à	until
C'est le comble!	That's the limit/last straw!
ça ne va pas	That won't do
du tout	at all
ou ... ou ...	either ... or ...

Dialogue

Desk clerk Je peux vous aider, madame?

Guest Oui. Il n'y a pas d'eau chaude.

Desk clerk Ah bon? C'est quelle chambre, madame?

Guest Trente-deux. Au quatrième étage – et l'ascenseur est toujours en panne!

Desk clerk Je vais envoyer quelqu'un tout de suite, madame.

Guest Et le téléviseur ne marche pas! Il pleut depuis mercredi et les enfants ne peuvent pas sortir...

Desk clerk Je vais essayer, mais aujourd'hui c'est difficile, madame. Si vous pouvez patienter jusqu'à lundi matin...

Guest Lundi matin? Oh, mais ça, c'est le comble! Non, ça ne va pas du tout. Ou vous me donnez un autre téléviseur ou je veux une autre chambre.

Desk clerk Très bien, madame. Si vous voulez je peux vous donner chambre 21 au premier étage.

Exercices

1 **Ecoutez!**
Listen to another guest complaining about his room and tick the correct answers. Remember the expression **en panne** from Unit 35. (*Answers on page 129.*)

a) The guest says the shower is broken _____ there is no shower _____.

b) The room number is 264 _____ 274 _____.

c) The second problem mentioned is the TV _____ the lift_____.

d) He will have to wait 30 minutes _____ till tomorrow _____.

2   Lisez! Ecrivez!
Here is another exchange between the hotel receptionist and an increasingly angry guest. Reassemble the jumbled up sentences in the most likely sequence and number them 1 to 9. (*Answers on page 129.*)

a) Au deuxième étage? Et l'ascenseur? Il est en panne depuis jeudi!   [   ]

b) Merci. Il pleut et les enfants veulent regarder la télévision.   [   ]

c) Oui, le téléviseur ne marche pas.   [   ]

d) Bonjour, monsieur. Il y a un problème?   [   ]

e) La semaine prochaine? Mais ça, c'est le comble!   [   ]

f) Les douches sont au deuxième étage, monsieur.[   ]

g) Je vais envoyer quelqu'un tout de suite, monsieur.   [   ]

h) Pour l'ascenseur il faut patienter jusqu'à mardi.   [   ]

i) Puis il n'y a pas de douche dans la chambre.   [   ]

3   ... et parlez français!
Re-create the dialogue at the reception desk using the prompts below. (*Answers on page 129.*) The receptionist starts by asking you if you have a problem.

1. The phone doesn't work.
2. 47 – on the 4th floor.
3. There's no water in the shower.
4. You've really had enough, now! You say 'This is the last straw – I want another room immediately, with TV and shower.'

En français

1. Note the irregular verb **vouloir** – 'to want'. You will find it in the Verb Tables on page 132 and after Exercise 3 on your recording.

2. *Ordinal numbers.* -**ième**, often written simply as -**e**, is the equivalent of the English 'nd', 'rd', 'th': **Au deuxième (2e) étage** – 'On the second floor'.

But note 'first' is **premier** (fem. **première**).

3. The **ou ... ou** construction means 'either ... or'.

> <u>Ou</u> vous me donnez un autre téléviseur <u>ou</u> je veux une autre chambre
> <u>Either</u> you give me another television <u>or</u> I want another room

En France

French hotels no longer require citizens of the **Union Européenne** to deposit their passports when they check in and formalities are generally kept to a minimum for tourists. Of course, you will still need your French to give (and possibly spell) your name, number of nights, number of people, car registration number, etc.

Numbers

At the insurance office

Vocabulaire

mil (m)	thousand (in dates)
naissance (f)	birth
espace (m)	space
valeur (f)	value
estimer	to estimate
tous risques	comprehensive (lit. 'all risks')
disons	let's say

Dialogue

Clerk	Votre date de naissance, s'il vous plaît.
Mr Morris	Mil neuf cent quarante-neuf.
Clerk	La marque et le modèle de votre véhicule?
Mr Morris	C'est une Renault 'Espace'.
Clerk	Le numéro d'immatriculation?
Mr Morris	N 389 PMW.
Clerk	Et l'année d'immatriculation?
Mr Morris	Mil neuf cent quatre-vingt-quinze.
Clerk	A combien estimez-vous la valeur de la voiture?
Mr Morris	Euh, disons quatre-vingt mille francs.
Clerk	Vous voulez tous risques?
Mr Morris	Oui.
Clerk	Ça fait mille neuf cent soixante-huit francs, monsieur. Vous payez par chèque ou carte de crédit?

Exercices

1   Ecoutez!

Listen to the dialogue again and tick the boxes VRAI or FAUX. (*Answers on page 130.*)

a) Mr Morris was born in 1949.
b) His car registration no. is N 399 PMW.
c) His car was registered in 1995.
d) His car's estimated value is 80,000 francs.
e) The insurance premium is 1978 francs.

VRAI	FAUX

2   Ecrivez!

Listen to the recording for Exercise 3 and write out in words the statistics given. (*Answers on page 130.*)

a) *Date of birth* le ....
b) *Type of car* Peugeot...
c) *Car registration no.* ....PXA ....
d) *Year of registration*..
e) *Estimated value* ....

3 ... et parlez français!
Now take the part of a customer in the insurance office, using the following details to answer the questions. (*Answers page 130.*)

Date of birth.............................29/3/56
Car registration no.............303 PXA 98
Estimated value.......................90.000F

Type of car ....Peugeot 506
Year of registration 1996
Type of insurance ....Comprehensive

En français

1.   **Dire** – 'to say', 'to tell'. Listen to the present tense of **dire** on your recording after Exercise 3. Remember all common irregular verbs used in this book are in the Verb Tables on pages 131–2.

2.   To say 'Let's', just omit the **nous** from the present tense of the verb following.

e.g.	**Nous disons**	We say	**Disons**	Let's say
	Nous voyons	We see	**Voyons**	Let's see
	Nous parlons	We speak	**Parlons français**	Let's speak French

3.   *Dates.* **Mille** is the usual word for 'thousand', but note that in dates it changes its spelling to **mil** (see dialogue). Another way of saying '1998' is **Dix-neuf cent quatre-vingt-dix-huit**.

En France

The cost of car insurance is high in France, especially in Paris, though for French motorists rates are lower if the policy – **la police** – is taken out through a professional or trades union (**un syndicat**, incidentally). Any kind of insurance is **l'assurance**, including life assurance which is **l'assurance-vie**. Visitors driving to France will need to have their **carte verte** (green card insurance certificate) and their **carte grise** (vehicle registration document) with them to show to the police – also **la police** in French – if required.

Talking about yourself

Past events

Vocabulaire

enfance (f)	childhood
étude (f)	study
université (f)	university
qui	who
normand	Norman
agréable	pleasant
déménager	to move (house)
rencontrer	to meet
se marier	to get married
rentrer	to come back
partir (irreg)	to leave, go away
quand	when
presque	almost, nearly
au bord de la mer	by the seaside
la semaine dernière	last week
j'y ai passé mon enfance	I spent my childhood there
J'en ai deux	I have two
Je suis allée le voir	I went to see him
je trouve	I find, I think
J'avais 15 ans	I was 15

Dialogue

Jean Vous êtes née ici?

Claire Non, je suis normande. Je suis née au bord de la mer, à Dieppe. J'y ai passé mon enfance. Quand j'avais 15 ans nous avons déménagé à Tours, où j'ai fait mes études à l'université.

Jean Et votre mari?

Claire Vincent est né à Toulouse. Il est venu à Tours pour son travail. Je l'ai rencontré en 1972 et nous nous sommes mariés en 1974.

Jean Vous habitez ici depuis longtemps?

Claire Depuis presque dix ans. Nous avons passé trois ans aux Etats-Unis, puis, quand nous sommes rentrés, nous avons décidé de rester à Tours. C'est une ville très agréable, je trouve.

Jean Vous avez des enfants?

Claire J'en ai deux. Brigitte, elle a 15 ans, et Jerôme, qui a 18 ans. Il est parti déjà. Il a trouvé un emploi à Rouen. Je suis allée le voir la semaine dernière.

Exercices

1 Ecoutez!

Listen again to the dialogue and tick the boxes at the top of the next page to indicate whether the following statements are true or false. (*Answers on page 130.*)

a) Claire was born in Dieppe.
b) She spent her childhood in Tours.
c) Her husband went to Toulouse to work.
d) He met Claire in 1972.
e) They spent ten years in the USA.

VRAI	FAUX

Cross reference with units:

2 Lisez! Ecrivez!
How would Vincent have given Jean the same details about himself and his wife Claire? For example, **Elle est née** instead of **Je suis née**. Revise the perfect tense in Units 27, 38 and 39 and refer to the **En français** section in this unit, then write in the missing words in the following sentences. (*Answers on page 130.*)

Ma femme est normande. Elle ___ née au bord de la mer. Elle a _____ son enfance à Dieppe. Ses parents ___ déménagé à Tours. Elle a ____ ses études à l'université. Je ____ venu à Tours pour mon travail. Nous nous sommes _____ en 1974.

3 ... et parlez français!
Re-create the dialogue, with yourself answering questions about your life, using the prompts below. (*Answers on page 130.*)

1. Say 'No, I'm Parisian.'
2. Explain that you came here when you were ten.
3. Tell her you went to the University of Nice in 1986 ...
4. Say 'No, I spent two years in England.'
5. Since 1992.

En français

1. A few verbs use **être**, not **avoir**, to form the *perfect tense*.

avoir		être	
J'ai passé	I spent	**Je suis allé(e)**	I went
Nous avons déménagé	We moved	**Nous sommes rentrés**	We returned

About a dozen verbs (Verb Tables, pages 131–2), use **être** in this way, as do all reflexive verbs, e.g. **se marier** in this unit. Also note that with **être** verbs, **-e** or **-s** is added if the subject is feminine or plural.

Elle s'est mariée	She (got) married
Nous nous sommes mariés	We (got) married

2. Note **y** – 'there'. It is placed *before* the verb.

J'y vais	I am going <u>there</u>	**Il y va**	He is going <u>there</u>
J'y ai passé mon enfance	I spent my childhood <u>there</u>		

3. A new past tense makes its appearance in this unit. **J'avais 15 ans** – I was 15. **Avais** is the *imperfect tense* of **avoir**. The imperfect tense will be dealt with in Units 58 and 59.

En France

As has been said, the French are traditionally attached to their **pays** and move house less readily than their British neighbours. If the parental home is not permanently occupied by the next generation it is often maintained as a **résidence secondaire** (second home), especially if it is **à la campagne** (in the country).

Out and about

Getting to the airport

Vocabulaire

illustré (m)	magazine
station de taxi (f)	taxi rank
aéroport (m)	airport
vol (m)	flight
pressé	in a hurry
lourd	heavy
monter	to get in
valoir (irreg)	to be worth
devoir (irreg)	to have to, must
pas grand-chose	not a lot
avant onze heures	before eleven o'clock
Que faire?	What shall I do?
il vaut mieux prendre	you'd better take
je dois être	I must be
Elle est à vous?	Is it yours?
Ouf!	Oh! Phew!
trois quarts d'heure	three-quarters of an hour
plus ou moins	more or less
Ça dépend (du trafic)	That depends (on the traffic)

Dialogues

1. Michèle Qu'est-ce que vous avez comme journaux?
Vendor Pas grand-chose, hein. *Le Monde, France-Soir, Nice-Matin* …
Michèle *Le Monde,* et un illustré … *Paris-Match.* Merci. Euh, l'autobus pour l'aéroport, il n'est pas encore arrivé?
Vendor Il est arrivé et il est parti il y a cinq minutes, mademoiselle. Et c'est le dernier avant onze heures.
Michèle Oh là là! J'ai un vol à midi. Que faire?
Vendor Il vaut mieux prendre un taxi. La station de taxi est là-bas, mademoiselle. De l'autre côté… Mademoiselle! Vous n'avez pas payé! Vingt-cinq francs, s'il vous plaît!

2. Michèle Je dois être à l'aéroport avant midi!
Taxi-driver Elle est à vous, cette valise?
Michèle Oui, oui, la verte.
Taxi-driver Ouf! Elle est lourde! Voilà. Montez, mademoiselle.
Michèle C'est loin, l'aéroport? Je suis très pressée.
Taxi-driver Trois quarts d'heure, plus ou moins. Ça dépend du trafic…

Exercices

1 Ecoutez!
Listen to another conversation at the newspaper kiosk and tick the correct information in the boxes at the top of the next page. (*Answers on page 130.*)

a) She buys *Le Monde* ☐ *Le Figaro* ☐ *Nice-Matin* ☐ *France-Soir* ☐.
b) The magazine bought is *Paris-Match* ☐ *L'Express* ☐ *Elle* ☐.
c) The paper and magazine cost 20F ☐ 22F ☐ 25F ☐.
d) The taxi rank is behind ☐ in front of ☐ next to ☐ the café.
e) The journey to the airport takes 15 ☐ 30 ☐ 45 ☐ minutes.

6
18
30
42

Cross reference with units:

2 Lisez!
When you are familiar with the dialogue to this unit, see if you can provide the questions for these answers – without looking at the text across the page!

a) _____ ? Pas grand-chose: *Le Monde,*
   _____ ? *France-Soir, Ouest-France.*
b) _____ ? Il vaut mieux prendre un taxi.
c) _____ ? Oui, la verte.
d) _____ ? Trois quarts d'heure, plus ou moins.

3 … et parlez français!
Now re-enact the first dialogue, at the newspaper kiosk, using the prompts below. (*Answers on page 130.*)

1. Say 'What English newspapers do you have?'
2. Ask for the *Guardian*. Ask for the *Le Figaro* as well.
3. Say 'No, thanks.' then 'Excuse me, I have to be at the airport at two o'clock. Is there a bus?'
4. Say thank you very much and ask how much it is for the newspapers.

En français

1. *The perfect tense.* **Arriver** and **partir** are two more verbs on the list of verbs forming this tense with **être** (see Unit 53).

| **Il est arrivé et il est parti** | It arrived and it left |

Refer to the Verb Tables on pages 131–2 and you will notice that all but three (**naître**, **mourir**, **rester**) have to do with *movement*.

2. Elsewhere, of course, **je suis**, **il est**, etc. retain their usual present tense meanings – 'I am', 'you are', 'he/she is', etc. **Elle est normande** – 'She is a Norman'; **Je suis pressé** – 'I am in a hurry'.

3. For 'mine', 'yours' etc., just say 'to me', 'to you' and so on.

| **Elle est à vous, cette valise?** | Is this suitcase *yours* (to you)? |
| **Oui, elle est à moi** | Yes, it's *mine* (to me) |

4. **Devoir** – 'to have to', a common alternative to **il faut**. See Verb Tables and listen to your recording after Exercise 3.

En France

Le Monde and *Le Figaro* are France's best known daily newspapers, but regional dailies with very large circulations such as *Ouest-France* for the west and *Nice-Matin* for the south-east of the country also carry national and international, as well as local news. *Paris-Match* is France's most popular weekly magazine.

Public transport

At the airport

Vocabulaire

bagages (m. pl)	baggage
renseignements (m. pl)	information
(non-)fumeur (m)	(non-) smoker
porte (f)	gate, door
embarquement (m)	boarding
prévu	scheduled, expected
prié	requested
faire enregistrer	to have (baggage) checked in
se présenter	to report
il partira	it will leave
en retard	late
ensemble	together

Dialogues

A Michèle — Je peux faire enregistrer mes bagages ici? Vol Médair 537 pour Londres.

Stewardess — Non, ce n'est pas ici, mademoiselle. Il faut demander aux Renseignements. De l'autre côté.

Michèle — Merci.

B Michèle — Le vol 537 est en retard?

Desk clerk — Oui, un peu.

Michèle — Quand est-ce qu'il partira?

Desk clerk — Attendez, mademoiselle, je vais vérifier. Alors départ prévu pour 19h30. Vous pouvez déjà faire enregistrer vos bagages.

C Stewardess — Votre passeport et votre billet, s'il vous plaît.

Michèle — Voilà. Vous avez deux places ensemble?

Stewardess — Oui, bien sûr. Fumeurs ou non-fumeurs?

Michèle — Non-fumeurs.

D Loudspeaker — Attention! Les passagers pour le vol 537 à destination de Londres sont priés de se présenter à la porte numéro 14 pour embarquement immédiat.

Exercices

1 Ecoutez!
Listen to these two airport announcements and fill in the missing details. (*Answers on page 130.*)

a) The message is for passengers on flight no. ___ travelling to _____. They are asked to report to gate __.

b) Passengers for flight ___ are asked to proceed to _____.

2 Lisez! Ecrivez!
Unscramble these sentences. (*Answers on page 130.*)

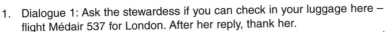

a) Vous ensemble plaît avez s'il places vous deux ?
b) aux faut madame Renseignements Il demander
c) ici enregistrer mes Je faire peux bagages ?
d) plaît Votre et passeport votre s'il billet vous

3 ... et parlez français!
Play the dialogues again. Stop the recording as necessary to speak the part of Michèle. Check your answers on the recording.

1. Dialogue 1: Ask the stewardess if you can check in your luggage here – flight Médair 537 for London. After her reply, thank her.
2. Dialogue 2: Ask the desk clerk if flight 537 is late. When he answers, ask when it will leave.
3. Dialogue 3: The stewardess asks for your passport and ticket. Say 'Here you are' and ask if she has two seats together.
4. She asks 'Smokers or non-smokers?' Answer 'Non-smokers'.

En français

The future. There are two ways of expressing the future.
Either a) Present tense of **aller** + the infinitive of the verb.

Je vais partir	I am going to leave
Nous allons téléphoner	We are going to phone

Or b) *Future tense* endings added to the infinitive of the verb. These are the same as the present tense endings of **avoir**.

-ai	-as	-a	-ons	-ez	-ont
Je partir<u>ai</u>				I shall leave	
Ils téléphoner<u>ont</u>				They will phone	

A few verbs form the future tense irregularly, e.g. **vous verrez** – 'You will see' (Unit 18). You will find some of them listed in the Verb Tables on pages 131–2.

En France

France's main passenger airport is Charles de Gaulle at Roissy, north of Paris, easily reached by the **A1** (**autoroute**) or by the fast **RER** rail link with the centre of Paris. 'Franglais' words such as **le check-in** and **le charter** are in common use at airports. At the check-in, as well as **votre billet** and **votre passeport** listen out for one other essential piece of paper you will be asked for – **votre carte d'embarquement, s'il vous plaît** – your boarding pass.

56 Shopping

In the bookshop

Dialogue

Denise	Est-ce que vous avez *Mille astuces pour le bricoleur*?
Assistant	Bricolage et jardinage au premier étage, madame. A côté de l'ascenseur.
Denise	Mais non, j'ai déjà cherché.
Assistant	Attendez, madame. Vous avez le nom de l'auteur?
Denise	Non, je ne sais pas. C'est une nouvelle édition.
Assistant	Ah oui, voilà. Je l'ai trouvé. Il vient d'être publié. Nous ne l'avons pas encore reçu. Si vous voulez repasser dans quelques semaines?
Denise	Merci, mais c'est pour mon mari. C'est son anniversaire lundi.
Assistant	Vous avez vu *Le Nouveau Manuel du bricolage* dans la vitrine? Il vient de paraître et il est en promotion en ce moment. Le voici, si vous voulez regarder, madame.
Denise	Oui, en effet. Il est très beau. Et à 75 francs c'est pas cher. Oui, d'accord, je le prends.

Exercices

1 Ecoutez!

Listen to two customers in the bookshop, then say whether the statements are true or false. Check the **En France** section before you start. (*Answers on page 130.*)

	VRAI	FAUX
a) The first customer wants a book on gardening.		
b) It is for his daughter's birthday.		

c) He gives the assistant the name of the author.

	VRAI	FAUX

Now the second customer.

	VRAI	FAUX
d)		
e)		
f)		

d) She asks about a particular love story.
e) She wants it as holiday reading.
f) She pays 69 francs for it.

2 Lisez! Ecrivez!

Use one of the words below to complete each of the phrases. (*Answers on page 130.*)

publié   reçu   regarder   trouvé   cherché

a) Non, j'ai déjà _____.
b) Il vient d'être _____.
c) Nous ne l'avons pas encore _____.
d) Oui, voilà, je l'ai _____.
e) Le voici, si vous voulez _____.

3 … et parlez français!

Play the dialogue again and speak the part of Denise, stopping the recording as necessary. Check your answers on the recording.

1. You start by asking the assistant if she has *Mille astuces pour le bricoleur.*
2. She suggests trying on the first floor. Say, I've already looked.'
3. She asks if you have the name of the author. Answer 'No, I don't know. It's a new edition.'
4. She suggests you call back in a few weeks. Say 'Thanks, but it's for my husband. It's his birthday on Monday.'
5. She shows you another book. Say 'Yes, indeed. It's very beautiful. And at 75 francs that's not expensive. Yes, OK, I'll take it.'

En français

Adjectives. A handful have irregular feminine and plural forms. You met **blanc** in Unit 32 and **beau** and **vieux** in Unit 49. **Nouveau** behaves in similar fashion. Here are the complete forms of these four adjectives.

Masculine		Feminine		
Sing.	*Plural*	*Sing.*	*Plural*	
nouveau	**nouveaux**	**nouvelle**	**nouvelles**	new
beau	**beaux**	**belle**	**belles**	beautiful, handsome
vieux	**vieux**	**vieille**	**vieilles**	old
blanc	**blancs**	**blanche**	**blanches**	white

En France

A bookshop is **une librairie**, while the town library, less important in France than in Britain as a social centre, is **la bibliothèque municipale**. The **librairie** will more often be a local or family business than a national chain store. Books are expensive but any bookshop will have its **Livre de Poche** and other paperback sections catering for, in particular, **le roman** (the novel) – perhaps a **roman policier** (detective story), **roman d'anticipation** (science fiction novel) or **roman d'amour** (love story).

Services
At the estate agent's

Vocabulaire

appartement (m)	flat, apartment
pièce (f)	room
loyer (m)	rent
rez-de-chaussée (m)	ground floor
immeuble (m)	building
chauffage central (m)	central heating
charges (f. pl)	maintenance/ service charges
salle de séjour (f)	living room
salle à manger (f)	dining room
cuisine équipée (f)	fitted kitchen
machine à laver (f)	washing machine
lave-vaisselle (m)	dishwasher
balcon (m)	balcony
adresse (f)	address
jardin (m)	garden
propriétaire (m/f)	owner, landlord/landlady
neuf (fem. **neuve**)	(brand-) new
modéré	moderate
tranquille	quiet
C'est un 4 pièces	It's a 4-room flat
donner sur	to look out on to
sera libre	will be free
par mois	per month
en plein centre-ville	right in the middle of town

PRINS IMMOBILIER

13-15, Rue de Calais

62500 ST-OMER

Pour vendre, acheter, louer

LA PASSION DE L'IMMOBILIER

21 98 36 00

Dialogue

Joël Mercier	Je cherche une maison ou un appartement à louer pour les vacances de Pâques.
Anne Delors	J'ai un très bel appartement à Neuilly qui sera libre à la fin du mois. C'est un 4 pièces au rez-de-chaussée d'un immeuble neuf. Il y a un petit jardin et un garage. Le loyer est très modéré – 1200F la semaine, toutes charges comprises.
Joël Mercier	Il y a combien de chambres?
Anne Delors	Attendez ... Deux chambres, salle de séjour avec balcon, salle à manger, chauffage central, cuisine équipée avec machine à laver et lave-vaisselle, WC et salle de bains.
Joël Mercier	Et c'est à Neuilly?
Anne Delors	Oui, en plein centre-ville mais l'appartement donne sur le parc et le quartier est très tranquille. Si vous voulez le voir, je téléphonerai au propriétaire ce soir.

Exercices

1 Ecoutez!
Play the dialogue again, listen carefully to the details and fill in the grid opposite. (*Answers on page 130.*)

Floor	No. of rooms	No. of bedrooms	TV Y/N	Washing machine Y/N	Dishwasher Y/N	Garage Y/N	Large garden Y/N	Rent

2 Lisez!

Read these two small ads for flats to let. Many of the key words are abbreviated. Can you work out the meanings? Refer to the **En France** section. (*Answers on page 130.*)

a) ***Appt 2 p. rue St Pierre. 3e ét. dans imm. nf. Ch. centr. balcon sud. 5000F/mois.***

b) This advertisement is for **un studio** – 'a bed sit'.
Charmant studio près ctre vlle. 40m2, r. de ch., balcon s. parc 2500F ch. comp.

3 ... et parlez français!

Re-create the dialogue at the estate agent's on the facing page. (*Answers on page 130.*) You start the conversation by saying what you are looking for.

1. 'I'm looking for a flat to let for two people in June'.
2. For two weeks.
3. Find out how much the rent is.
4. Ask if there is a washing machine.
5. Ask if you can see the flat today.

En français

1. The irregular adjectives **beau**, **nouveau**, **vieux**, which you met in the last unit, have special masculine forms **bel**, **nouvel**, **vieil** when followed by a noun beginning with a vowel or silent **h**.

un beau magasin	**un bel immeuble**
un vieux café	**un vieil hôtel**

Note that **vieil** is pronounced like **vieille** (see Unit 49).

2. Note **nouveau** is the usual word for 'new' but **neuf** is used in the sense of 'brand new', 'just made/built'.

3. Two more verbs in the *future tense* in this dialogue: one regular, from **téléphoner**, and one irregular, from **être** ('to be').

Je téléphonerai	I *will* phone	**qui sera**	which *will* be

Note the future of regular **-IR** and **-RE** verbs.

Je finirai	I will finish	**Je descendrai**	I will get down

En France

The **petites annonces** (small ads) of a French newspaper or in the window of the local **agent immobilier** (estate agent) will confirm the fact that the French are still, by and large, apartment dwellers. If you are flat hunting it is important to know the surface area and the number of rooms (**pièces**), excluding kitchen and bathroom, also which floor (**étage**) the flat is on. To the rent (**le loyer**) add the **charges**, unless they are already allowed for (**comprises**). These will include such items as maintenance and security of the building, and services provided by the **concierge** (caretaker), who is also called **le gardien**.

Eating out

Settling the bill

agneau (m)	lamb
erreur (f)	error, mistake
mère (m)	mother
cognac (m)	cognac, brandy
excellent	excellent
nature	black (coffee)
terminer	to finish
c'était	it was

Dialogue

Waitress	Vous avez terminé, messieurs-dames? Vous avez bien mangé?
Guy	Excellent.
Béatrice	L'agneau était délicieux.
Guy	Mais je crois qu'il y a une erreur sur l'addition. Vous avez mis 180F pour les escargots. Sur la carte c'était 60F.
Waitress	Oui, monsieur. C'est 60F la douzaine. Vous avez pris les escargots pour trois personnes, n'est-ce pas?
Guy	Non, pour deux seulement. Ma mère a pris les moules.
Waitress	Ah bon? Oui, en effet, excusez-moi, monsieur.
Guy	C'est pas grave.
Waitress	Je vais changer ça tout de suite. Vous prenez un café? Un digestif?
Béatrice	Juste un petit café pour moi. Nature.
Guy	Pour moi, un cognac. Maman, pour toi? Rien?
Waitress	Alors un café et un cognac. Merci, messieurs-dames.

Exercices

1 Ecoutez!

The waiter is making some mistakes as he checks these bills. Listen carefully, refer to the actual items ordered below and put a cross by each one he has got wrong. (*Answers on page 130.*)

a) 2 mushroom soups
   1 steak and chips
   1 roast chicken
   2 strawberry tarts
   1 white coffee
   1 tea

b) 1 mussels in white wine
   1 green salad
   2 chicken in wine
   1 cheese
   1 cake
   2 black coffees
   1 brandy

2 Lisez! Ecrivez!

Choose an appropriate word or phrase from the list below to complete the six sentences on the next page. (*Answers on page 130.*)

cognac   **moules**   **tout de suite**   **l'addition**   **mangé**   **délicieux**

a) Il y a une erreur sur _____. b) Vous avez bien _____?
c) Alors un café et un _____. d) Je vais changer ça _____.
e) L'agneau était _____. f) Ma mère a pris les _____.

3 ... et parlez français!
You have ordered menu a) from Exercise 1, but there is a mistake
in the bill. Point it out when the waitress comes, using the prompts below.
(*Answers on page 130.*)

1. Say 'Yes, the chicken was delicious.'
2. But there's a mistake on the bill.
3. Tell her she's put 55 francs for the steak, but on the menu it was 45.
4. Say 'Don't worry about it.'
5. Order two coffees and a brandy.

En français

1. *The imperfect tense.* Used to describe *how things were* – e.g. where you used
to live, or what something was like, what someone's age or the weather or time of
day was.

C'était délicieux It was delicious   **J'avais 15 ans** I was 15

For this tense the commonest endings are **-ais** (for **je** and **tu**) and **-ait** (for **il** and
elle). You will find all the endings in the Verb Tables on pages 131–2.

2. But remember always to use the *perfect tense* for a *single past action or
event*.

J'ai téléphoné I phoned   **Elle a bu le café** She drank the coffee
Il est venu He came   **Ils sont retournés** They returned

3. The verbs **mettre** (to put) and **prendre** (to take) are irregular in the perfect
tense, with the past participle ending in **-is**.

Ma mère a pris (took/has taken)   **Vous avez mis** (put/have put)

4. Note **pour toi** – for you. The formal equivalent is **pous vous**.

En France

A **digestif** – a **cognac** or liqueur – drunk with a strong black coffee is the
traditional way to round off the evening meal in a French restaurant. Incidentally,
remember not to call the waiter or waitress '**Garçon!**' or '**Serveuse!**' but, should
you need to call them over to your table, '**Monsieur**', '**Mademoiselle**' or
'**Madame**'.

Travel by car

Ferry or tunnel?

Vocabulaire

week-end (m)	weekend
offre (f)	offer
avion (m)	plane
tunnel (m)	tunnel
fois (f)	time
ferry (m)	ferry
conducteur (m)	driver
passager (m)	passenger
occasion (f)	bargain
spécial	special
calme	calm
pas mal	not bad
puisque	since
insister	to insist
avoir envie (**de**)	to feel like
avoir le mal de mer	to be seasick
avoir peur (**de**)	to be afraid (of)
le voici	here it is
On y va!	Let's go!

Dialogue

Janine   Jacques! Tu as vu le journal?

Jacques   Oui, il était dans la cuisine. Je le lisais ce matin. Pourquoi?

Janine   Parce que j'ai envie de passer un week-end à Londres! Il y a une offre spéciale pour le ferry la semaine prochaine.

Jacques   Moi, je préfère l'avion, ou bien le tunnel. L'année dernière nous avons pris le ferry et j'ai eu le mal de mer. Une heure et demie, c'est trop long.

Janine   Mais l'avion, c'est trop cher et tu sais bien que j'ai peur du tunnel. Et puis en juillet la mer sera calme. Ah, le voici, le journal. Regarde, Jacques.

Jacques   Quelle est cette offre spéciale, alors? Cinq cents francs pour la voiture, le conducteur et trois passagers … Oui, oui, c'est pas mal.

Janine   C'est une occasion.

Jacques   Bon, d'accord. Puisque tu insistes! On y va!

Exercices

1   **Ecoutez!**

Listen to this conversation about a trip to New York and tick the boxes as appropriate. (*Answers on page 130.*)

a) The offer is for Christmas ☐ Easter ☐ .

b) The offer is for 3 ☐ 4 ☐ 5 ☐ nights in New York.

c) Departure date is December 23rd ☐ 24th ☐ 25th ☐ .

d) The price is 1500F ☐ 2500F ☐ 3500F ☐ .

e) Accommodation is room only ☐ half board ☐ full board ☐ .

2 Lisez! Ecrivez!
Read the **En français** section in this unit and in Unit 58, then fill in the blanks with a suitable verb in the *perfect* or *imperfect* tense from those given below. (*Answers on page 130.*)

regardait   suis sorti(e)   lisais   avons déménagé   étais   avais

a) Je _____ le journal quand Jean-Pierre est entré.
b) J'avais 12 ans quand nous _____.
c) J'_____ peur du ferry quand j'_____ petit.
d) Elle _____ la télévision quand je suis arrivé.
e) Il faisait froid quand je _____.

3 ... et parlez français!
Play the dialogue again. Stop the recording as necessary to speak the part of Jacques. Check your answers on the recording.

1. Janine is looking for the newspaper. Say 'Yes, it was in the kitchen. I was reading it this morning. Why?'
2. She suggests the ferry next week. Say that you prefer the plane, or else the tunnel. Add 'Last year we took the ferry and I was sea-sick. One and a half hours is too long.'
3. She hands you the paper. Say 'What is this special offer, then? 500 francs for the car, the driver and 3 passengers. Yes, yes, that's not bad.'
4. Finally, say 'Good, agreed. Since you insist. Let's go.'

En français

1. *The imperfect tense.* A second use for this tense is to say that someone *was doing* something (when something else happened).

> **Je lisais le journal quand elle a téléphoné**
> I was reading the paper when she phoned

Refer to the Verb Tables on pages 131–2 and note that imperfect endings **-ais**, **-ait**, **-aient** are all pronounced the same.

2. *Expressions with **avoir**.* You have already seen how the verb **avoir** is used to give someone's age (Unit 17) and to talk about aches and pains (Unit 33). In this unit note two more common expressions with **avoir**.

J'ai envie de	I feel like spending (lit. I
passer un week-end	have the wish to spend) a weekend
J'ai peur du tunnel	I'm afraid of (lit. I have fear of) the tunnel

En France

Visitors to France from Great Britain can choose to take the plane (**l'avion**), or travel with or without their car by **le ferry** (ferryboat), **l'aéroglisseur** (hovercraft), or by shuttle train through **le Tunnel sous** (under) **la Manche** (the English Channel). At the customs – **la douane** – drivers and passengers will need to show their **passeport**. And just one more name to learn – if you cross via Dover the French name for this port is **Douvres**. So, finally, have a good trip – **Bon voyage! ... et parlez français!**

Language extra

These exercises provide extra practice in some of the important language skills you have learnt in Units 38–59. Check your answers on page 130.

A. The perfect tense

Remember: The perfect tense is used to say that something *happened once* in the past. Change the following from present to past by using the perfect tense.

e.g. Je téléphone à l'hôtel   J'ai téléphoné à l'hôtel.

1   Je réserve une chambre   _____
2   Nous prenons l'autoroute   _____
3   Nous arrivons à 7h30   _____
4   Marc stationne la voiture   _____
5   J'entre dans l'hôtel   _____

B. The imperfect tense

Remember: The imperfect tense is for something that *used to be* OR *used to happen regularly* OR for something that *was happening*. Change the following from present to past by using the imperfect tense.

e.g. J'habite à Bordeaux   J'habitais à Bordeaux.

1   Je lis mon journal   _____
2   Jean a envie d'aller à Paris   _____
3   Je travaille comme journaliste.   _____
4   Ils ont peur du tunnel   _____
5   C'est délicieux!   _____

C The future tense

The sentences below (taken from Exercise A) have been changed to the future by using **aller**. Express the same idea by using the future tense of the verb as in the example.

e.g. Je vais téléphoner à l'hôtel   Je téléphonerai à l'hôtel

1   Je vais réserver une chambre   _____
2   Nous allons prendre l'autoroute.   _____
3   Nous allons arriver à 7h30   _____
4   Marc va stationner la voiture.   _____
5   Je vais entrer dans l'hôtel.   _____

D Adjectives

Remember: Most adjectives *follow* the noun they describe and add **-e** or **-s** to 'agree' with a feminine or plural noun:

e.g. **une région française**   a French region

How would you say the following in French?
1 The blue sea   **La** _____.   2 A green salad   **Une** _____.
3 A direct train   **Un** _____.   4 Roast chicken   **Du** _____.

Remember: **Beau, nouveau, vieux** have irregular feminine and plural forms. These and a few other common adjectives, e.g. **grand, petit, bon, mauvais, jeune, joli, premier, deuxième** (etc.), **prochain, dernier,** *precede* the noun.

e.g. **Les premiers jours**   The first days

How would you say the following in French?
1 A small boy   **Un** _____   2 A young woman   **Une** _____.
3 The old towns   **Les** _____   3 The next train   **Le** _____

Testez-vous!

Test yourself to see how much you can remember from Units 38–59. Check your answers on the recording.

In French how would you...

1. Ask 'Can I have the bill?'
2. Ask 'How is that spelt?'
3. Say 'I have rented a farmhouse.'
4. Ask 'What is he/she like?
5. Say 'in spring; in summer; in autumn; in winter'.
6. Say 'in May; in July; in September'.
7. Say 'Excuse me, Officer' to a policeman.
8. Say 'I am/We are getting off at Nantes.'
9. Say 'Can I help you with your case?'
10. Say 'The French are difficult to know.'
11. Say 'Pleased to make your acquaintance.'
12. Say 'The lift is broken.'
13. Say 'I am in a hurry.'
14. Ask: 'Do you have two places together?'
15. Say 'I've found it.'
16. Say 'The lamb was delicious.'
17. Say 'I'm afraid of the tunnel.'
18. Say 'It's a bargain.'
19. Say 'It's not bad.'
20. Say 'Long live France!'

Answers

UNIT 1 **1** a) Faux; b) Vrai; c) Faux; d) Vrai; e) Faux; f) Vrai **2** Bonsoir; Je suis; Londres; Monsieur; Vous êtes; français **3** Je suis américaine. Je suis de New York. Je suis anglais. Je suis de Londres. Je suis italienne. Je suis de Rome.

UNIT 2 **1** Kir is not mentioned **2** Un café; Une bière; Deux cocas; Un kir; Trois oranges pressées **3** Deux cocas, s'il vous plaît/Un crème et deux bières./Pression, s'il vous plaît.

UNIT 3 **1** 1) single/shower/1 night/room no. 2; 2) double/bath/2 nights/room no. 3; 3) double/shower/1 night/room no. 4 **2** chambre/nuits/deux/douche/plaît **3** a) Bonsoir/Vous avez une chambre libre?/Pour deux personnes/Avec douche/Pour deux nuits/Très bien/Merci; b) Bonsoir/Vous avez une chambre libre?/Pour une personne/Avec bain/Pour quatre nuits/Très bien/Merci.

UNIT 4 **1** a) 11; 9; 23; 18; 17; 22; 16; b) Il est 5h/8h10/9h/10h20/11h15 **2** a) 2h12; b) 6h22; c) 9h05; d) 4h15; e) 9h14; f) 6h45; g) 10h50 **3** Il est a) trois heures; b) sept heures; c) midi; d) huit heures vingt-cinq; e) onze heures quinze.

UNIT 5 **1** White/English/lives in Watford/ works in Luton; Christine/French; Taylor/from New York/lives in Bath/works in Bristol; Gina/Italian/from Rome **2** a) Vous parlez très bien français, monsieur. b) Vous venez de Paris? c) Je parle français avec la famille. d) Je viens de Nice mais mon mari est parisien.

UNIT 6 **1** A) bar; B) café; C) bistro **2** a) iii; b) i; c) iv; d) v; e) ii **3** Pardon, monsieur./ Est-ce qu'il y a un restaurant près d'ici?/Non, j'ai une voiture./Merci, monsieur.

UNIT 7 **1** a) single/11.14; b) Paris/ 16.15/platform 9/110F; c) single/7h10/platform 12/118F **2** a) Je voudrais un aller simple pour Paris. b) Il arrive à quelle heure, s'il vous plaît? c) Je vous en prie, monsieur.

d) Le prochain train part à quelle heure? **3** Un aller simple pour Paris, s'il vous plaît./Le prochain train part à quelle heure?/Il arrive à Paris à quelle heure?/C'est direct?/Merci beaucoup. (Price 115F; dep. 19h05, arr. 20h10; platform 8)

UNIT 8 **1** 2 kilos, 5F60/200 g, 6F40/1 dozen, 10F30 **2** Crossword: Je voudrais trois cents grammes d'olives vertes, s'il vous plaît. **3** Deux kilos de tomates, s'il vous plaît./Je voudrais trois artichauts./Une douzaine d'œufs./C'est combien, les olives?/ Alors, donnez-moi deux cents grammes d'olives, s'il vous plaît. (The shopping cost 52F.)

UNIT 9 **1** puppets/Thursday 18.00/ 20.00 folk concert/Sunday 19.00 **2** a) Je reste à Nice jusqu'à vendredi. b) Ce soir il y a un concert à sept heures. c) Mardi il y a un cirque pour les enfants. d) Jeudi il y a un spectacle de marionnettes. **3** A) Est-ce que vous avez un programme des spectacles, s'il vous plaît?/Jusqu'à mercredi./Est-ce qu'il y a quelque chose ce soir? B) Un plan de la ville, s'il vous plaît./Une semaine./Merci. Est-ce qu'il y a quelque chose pour les enfants?

UNIT 10 **1** Man: fish/water/no dessert; Woman: steak/wine/dessert **2** a) Une carafe de vin rouge. b) Pour moi, un filet de sole. c) Je n'aime pas le poisson. **3** Un steak-frites, s'il vous plaît./Bient cuit, s'il vous plaît./Un pichet de vin rouge./Non, je ne prends pas de dessert.

UNIT 11 **1** a) Faux; b) Faux; c) Vrai; d) Vrai **2** a) dix-huit; vingt-quatre; trente-deux; trente-six; quarante et un; soixante; cent cinquante-six; deux cent dix; b) Crossword Across: 4) plein; 5) francs; 7) ici; 9) monnaie; 10) super; 11) libre; 12) sans. Down: 1) station; 2) caisse; 3) litres; 4) payer; 6) s'il; 8) vous **3** Faites le plein, s'il vous plaît./Oui, sans plomb./Je peux payer par carte de crédit?/Merci. Au revoir.

UNIT 12 **1** a) ii; b) iii; c) v; d) iv; e) i **2** a) Paris est une ville touristique. b) Je suis né dans le 11e arrondissement. c) Paris, c'est la ville où je travaille. d) Les Parisiens quittent leur ville pour aller en vacances.

UNIT 13 **A** Regular: 1) habitons; 2) parle; 3) arrive; 4) désirez; 5) pensent; 6) travaille; 7) parle; 8) habite; 9) tournez; 10) travaillons. Irregular: 1) viens; 2) avez; 3) êtes; 4) sommes; 5) est; 6) prends; 7) peux; 8) vais; 9) venez; 10) fait **B** 1) Donnez; 2) Faites; 3) Tournez; 4) Allez; 5) Prenez; 6) Signez **C** 1) Je ne parle pas bien. 2) Je n'aime pas Londres. 3) Je ne suis pas américain(e). 4) Je ne travaille pas ici. 5) Je ne suis pas en vacances.

UNIT 14 **1** Ordered: lemon tea/ham sandwich/apple tart **2** a) 23F50; b) 42F60; c) 6F50; d) 15F00; e) 49F50; f) 24F00 **3** Une bière et un thé au citron./Vous avez quelque chose à manger?/Qu'est-ce que vous avez comme sandwichs?/Je préfère le fromage./Et je voudrais une tarte aux fraises.

UNIT 15 **1** a) 350F; b) bathroom; c) 3rd floor; d) 30F; e) in front **2** a) ii; b) iv; c) v; d) vi; e) i; f) iii **3** Je voudrais une chambre pour deux personnes, s'il vous plaît./C'est un peu cher./Oui, ça va. Le petit déjeuner est compris?/Est-ce qu'il y a un parking?

UNIT 16 **1** 61; 70; 71; 75; 77; 80; 85; 91; 96; 98 **2** 02 21 03 89/61 93 37 86/81 17 80 99/52 11 34 76 **3** Check writing in Unit 16 vocabulary.

UNIT 17 **1** Céline Blanc: single/secretary/ 19; Jules Forget: French/married/chemist/45; Laure Simon: French/bank employee/34; Jean Camus: Swiss/divorced/42/daughter, 18 **2** Camus/Jean/professeur/suisse/Paris/ divorcé.

UNIT 18 **1** 72/20 mins/behind hotel/3F/ opposite/station/in front of you/1 p.m. **2** a) iv; b) i; c) v; d) ii; e) iii **3** Pardon, mademoiselle./Pour aller à l'Hôtel Mercure, s'il vous plaît?/ Non, nous sommes à pied./Ils sont fréquents, les autobus?/Où est le café?

UNIT 19 **1** a) 13.22; b) 15.34; c) 16.08; d) 16.49; e) 9 and 11; f) 92F each; g) 552F

2 Crossword. Across: 3) TGV; 6) correspon-dance; 7) demi; 8) TEE. Down: 1) place; 2) changer; 3) tarifs; 4) rapide; 5) réduit **3** Je peux réserver des places ici?/St-Etienne./Deux adultes et trois enfants./ Il y a un tarif réduit pour les enfants?/ Six ans, huit ans et onze ans.

UNIT 20 **1** a) watch; b) Japan, c) too expensive; d) bracelet; e) 430F **2** a) cette; b) c'est; c) celui; d) celle; e) ce **3** Est-ce que je peux voir cette montre, s'il vous plaît?/ Non, celle-là./Elle est très jolie. Elle coûte combien?/ Quel dommage! C'est trop cher./Je peux voir ce bracelet?/C'est quel prix?/Il me plaît beaucoup. Oui, je le prends.

UNIT 21 **1** 1) 1 letter to United States/5F60; 2) 2 postcards to Italy/6F40; 3) 1 parcel to England/13F20 **2** Crossword. Across: Portugal; Londres. Down: Allemagne; Espagne; Rome; Italie.

UNIT 22 **1** A) Aperitif ✓ Starter ✓; B) Aperitif ✗ Starter ✗; C) Aperitif ✓ Starter ✗ **2** a) Crudités; b) Dubonnet; c) Pernod; d) Escargots; e) Salade mixte; f) Pastis; g) Moules marinière **3** Est-ce que vous avez une table pour quatre personnes, s'il vous plaît?/ Un pastis, deux kirs et un jus d'orange (une orange pressée)/Moules, escargots, soupe à l'oignon, salade mixte.

UNIT 23 **1** A) Volkswagen Golf/2 days/ 300F; B) Peugeot 106/1 week/240F; C) Citroën ZX/2 days/280F **2** a) Je voudrais louer une voiture pour trois jours. b) Je préfère quelque chose de plus petit. c) A partir de lundi prochain. d) Il me faut votre permis de conduire et une pièce d'identité. **3** Je voudrais louer une voiture pour demain./Une grande. Nous sommes quatre adultes./Est-ce que vous avez quelque chose de moins cher?/Vous acceptez les cartes de crédit?

UNIT 24 **1** Mme Clair: Est; M. Simon: Sud; Mlle Drut: Ouest; M. Monet: Nord **2** a) Faux; b) Faux; c) Vrai; d) Vrai **3** Oui, je suis né à Leeds, dans le Nord./ Ma femme est française. Elle vient de Grasse, en Provence./ Nous habitons à Bristol, dans l'Ouest./Oui, je suis née à Miami, dans le Sud./ Nous habitons à Philadelphie, dans L'Est.

25 1 a) 25/Nice/Paris/secretary; b) 30/London/2/teacher 2 a) ii; b) iv; c) v; d) i; e) iii 3 Je m'appelle Jean-Pierre./J'ai quinze ans./J'habite à Grenoble./J'ai une sœur aînée./Elle s'appelle Sabine./Elle a vingt et un ans./Oui, elle est professeur.

26 1 a) Georges; b) chocolate; c) ham; d) 39F40; e) in the basement 2 a) chaud/lait; b) vais/attendant; c) chéri; d) téléphones/sous-sol 3 Une pression et une orange pressée./Et trois cartes postales./Où est le téléphone, s'il vous plaît?/ Et je voudrais une télécarte pour vingt francs.

27 1 Calais/Paris/Marseille/New York/Bordeaux 2 (See dialogue) 3 Je voudrais confirmer une réservation./Je m'appelle Jenkins. Je l'épelle – JENKINS./Oui, c'est ça. J'ai téléphoné lundi./Vers six heures.

28 1 8.30/9.45/7.25/9.15/12.00 2 b) cinq heures vingt; c) six heures et quart; d) huit heures et demie; e) minuit moins le quart.

29 1 Vrai/Faux/Faux/Faux/Vrai 2 préféré/piscine/samedis/paresseux/déteste/ joue/guitare/vendredis/danser/copains (copines) 3 Oui, j'aime beaucoup le tennis./Non, je n'aime pas la gymnastique, je déteste la gymnastique./Oui, j'aime jouer du piano./J'aime beaucoup sortir avec mes copains (copines if *all* feminine).

30 1 Paris – rain; Rouen – wind and cloud; Grenoble – sun; Perpignan – sun and storms 2 a) iv; b) v; c) i; d) ii; e) iii 3 Non, il fait mauvais./Je viens de téléphoner./ Oui, il pleut./Non, il fait très froid.

31 1 a) Vrai; b) Faux; c) Faux; d) Vrai 2 a) 9F; b) 48F; c) 150F; d) buses.

32 1 blouse/white or blue/blue/ on the left/36/big/skirt/550F/credit card 2 Horizontal: CLAIR, BLEU; ROSE; BLANC; COULEUR. Vertical: VERT; CHER; JUPE; ROBE 3 Ce pantalon, vous l'avez en d'autres couleurs?/

Je fais du … Il coûte combien?/Est-ce que je peux essayer le bleu?/Dommage. Il est trop petit. Avez-vous la taille au-dessus?/Oui, il me plaît. Je le prends.

33 1 A) headache and temperature/ tablets/3 a day with meals; B) bad stomach ache/pills/1 every 4 hours after meals/come back Monday if not better 2 a) gorge; b) fièvre; c) comprimés; d) ventre; e) dents; f) repas.

34 1 A) fish, tomatoes, chips; B) tomatoes, olives, French beans; C) chicken, wine, carrots, mushrooms 2 A) salade mixte, poulet rôti, haricots verts, vin blanc B) moules marinière, filet de sole, pommes frites, eau minérale 3 Une salade verte et des fruits de mer, s'il vous plaît./Le coq au vin, qu'est-ce que c'est?/Je n'aime pas tellement le poulet./Un filet de sole et un steak frites./Une carafe de vin blanc et un verre d'eau minérale.

35 1 Lusson/clutch/Peugeot/405/ red/1994/Guyot 2 a) iv; b) iii; c) v; d) vi; e) i; f) vii; g) ii 3 Je suis en panne./Je suis devant l'Hôtel Splendide à Avallon./Je ne sais pas. Je pense que c'est l'embrayage./C'est une Renault seize./Noire./Quatre-vingt-quatorze.

36 1 a) Faux; b) Faux; c) Vrai; d) Faux 2 meilleur/moins/meilleurs/plus 3 Oui, mais en Bourgogne il fait plus chaud/il y a moins de touristes/la cuisine est meilleure/les vins sont moins chers.

37 A 1) Oui, je la connais. 2) Oui, je l'aime. 3) Oui, vous la quittez. 4) Oui, nous l'avons visité. 5) Oui, je les connais. B 1a) J'ai réservé la chambre. b) Je vais réserver la chambre. 2a) Il a téléphoné à Nice. b) Il va téléphoner à Nice. 3a) Nous avons décidé. b) Nous allons décider. 4a) J'ai présenté mon ami. b) Je vais présenter mon ami. 5a) Vous avez essayé le pantalon? b) Vous allez essayer le pantalon? C Numbers: soixante-dix; soixante et onze; soixante-dix-neuf; quatre-vingt-deux; quatre-vingt-dix; quatre-vingt-dix-neuf; cent; cent cinquante; cinq cent soixante-dix. Times: trois heures; quatre heures cinq; six heures et demie; dix heures moins le quart **D** en France/en Espagne/au Portugal/en Suisse/ en Angleterre/aux Etats-Unis/au Canada/en Italie/en Normandie/en Allemagne/en Bretagne/en Provence.

U N I T 38 **1** Ordered: red wine/white coffee/ham sandwich/salami pizza/prawn pancake/draught beer/lemon tea/apple tart **2** J'ai: payé l'addition; bu ma bière; téléphoné à l'hôtel; réservé la chambre; fini de manger **3** Oui, j'ai payé l'addition/Oui, j'ai téléphoné à l'hôtel./Oui, j'ai réservé la chambre./Oui, j'ai bu ma bière.

U N I T 39 **1** Bastiani, Maria/italienne/2/4/6 Sep/9 Sep **2** (See dialogue).

U N I T 40 **1** 17/vii/89; 22/viii/47; 1/ix/92; 31/xii/55; 11/ii/97; 21/iii/89 **2** Crossword. Across: Août/Février/Avril/Juillet/Septembre/Janvier/Octobre. Down: Juin/Mai/Mars/Décembre/Novembre.

U N I T 41 **1** Anne: tall/long/contact lenses/casually/active; Marc: short/formally/glasses/older **2** Pierre: grand/mince/lunettes; Lucie: cheveux blonds/yeux bleus; Henri: costume élégant/chemise bleue/cravate noire.

U N I T 42 **1** 1) Keep moving; 2) No U-turns; 3) No parking here; 4) Free meter available; 5) Drive straight on; 6) Park across the street **2** a) iii; b) i; c) iv; d) v; e) ii **3** Pardon, monsieur l'agent./Est-ce qu'il y a un parking près d'ici?/Est-ce que c'est loin?/Je peux faire demi-tour?

U N I T 43 **1** a) Faux; b) Vrai; c) Faux; d) Vrai **2** (See dialogue).

U N I T 44 **1** A) 200 g salami/4 slices ham/100 g olives; B) 200 g olives/1 piece cheese **2** a) iii; b) iv; c) i; d) v; e) ii **3** Je voudrais un morceau de gruyère. Trois cents grammes./Je voudrais des olives noires./Cent cinquante./Et de la salade de riz, s'il vous plaît./Deux cents grammes./De la tête de veau, s'il vous plaît./Trois tranches./C'est tout, merci.

U N I T 45 **1** Cash a Eurocheque/Aug. 3/figures/7F40/No. 2 **2** a) changer; b) Ecrivez; c) Passez; d) encaisser; e) Donnez; f) retirer **3** Je voudrais changer de l'argent./J'ai cent cinquante livres./Quel est le cours de la livre?/Et la commission, c'est combien?

U N I T 46 **1** 1 salade verte, 1 salade mixte; 1 steak frites, 1 entrecôte; 2 haricots verts; 1 tarte aux pommes, 1 glace; 1 bouteille de Beaujolais **2** Entrée: fruits de mer; moules marinière; soupe à l'oignon. Plat principal: filet de sole; poulet rôti; choucroute garnie. Légumes: haricots verts; petits pois; pommes frites. Dessert: glace aux fraises; mousse au chocolat; tarte aux abricots. **3** Une moules marinière et deux fruits de mer./Un poulet rôti, un steak frites et un filet de sole./Des haricots verts et des petits pois./Une mousse au chocolat, une glace aux fraises et une tarte aux abricots.

U N I T 47 **1** a) lead-free petrol; b) 92F40; c) water; d) major road **2** Avancez un peu/Faites le plein/Ouvrez le capot/Donnez-moi la clé/Prenez l'autoroute **3** Faites le plein. Super sans plomb, s'il vous plaît./Voilà. Pouvez-vous vérifier l'huile, s'il vous plaît?/Pour aller à Calais, je prends l'autoroute ou la N quarante-trois?/Merci. Au revoir.

U N I T 48 **1** a) Faux; b) Faux; c) Vrai; d) Vrai; e) Faux **2** No set answers.

U N I T 49 **1** a) Faux; b) Faux; c) Faux; d) Vrai; e) Vrai **2** No set answers.

U N I T 50 **1** a) pièces; b) 00; c) code; d) Hold on; e) Allô!; f) Comment allez-vous? **2** mettez/composez/attendez/quittez **3** Allô! Je voudrais parler à Monsieur Cléry, s'il vous plaît./Bonjour, Monsieur Cléry. Je suis … Comment allez-vous?

U N I T 51 **1** a) shower broken; b) 274; c) lift; d) 30 mins **2** 1) d; 2) c; 3) g; 4) b; 5) i; 6) f; 7) a; 8) h; 9) e **3** Le téléphone ne marche pas./Quarante-sept, au quatrième étage./Et il n'y a pas d'eau dans la douche./Mais ça, c'est le comble! Je veux une autre chambre, tout de suite, avec télévision et douche.

52 1 a) vrai; b) faux; c) vrai; d) vrai; e) faux 2 a) vingt-neuf mars mil neuf cent cinquante six; b) cinq cent six; c) trois cent trois; quatre-vingt-dix-huit; d) mil neuf cent quatre-vingt-seize; e) quatre-vingt-dix mille 3 le vingt-neuf mars mil neuf cent cinquante-six/C'est une Peugeot cinq cent six./trois cent trois PXA quatre-vingt-dix-huit/mil neuf cent quatre-vingt-seize/quatre-vingt-dix mille/Oui.

53 1 a) Vrai; b) Faux; c) Faux; d) Vrai; e) Faux 2 est/passé/ont/fait/suis/mariés 3 Non, je suis parisien(ne)./Je suis venu(e) ici quand j'avais dix ans./Je suis allé(e) à l'université de Nice en mil neuf cent quatre-vingt-six./Non, j'ai passé deux ans en Angleterre./Depuis mil neuf cent quatre-vingt-douze.

54 1 a) *Nice-Matin*; b) *Express*; c) 22F; d) in front; e) 30 2 (See dialogue) 3 Qu'est-ce que vous avez comme journaux anglais?/Le *Guardian*, s'il vous plaît. Et je voudrais *Le Figaro* aussi./Non, merci. Euh, pardon, monsieur. Je dois être à l'aéroport à deux heures. Est-ce qu'il y a un bus?/Merci beaucoup. C'est combien pour les journaux?

55 1 a) 738/New York/16; b) 295/check-in 2 a) Vous avez deux places ensemble, s'il vous plaît? b) Il faut demander aux Renseignements, madame. c) Je peux faire enregistrer mes bagages ici? d) Votre billet et votre passeport, s'il vous plaît.

56 1 1st: a) Vrai; b) Faux; c) Faux. 2nd: d) Faux; e) Vrai; f) Vrai 2 a) cherché; b) publié; c) reçu; d) trouvé; e) regarder.

57 1 Ground/4/2/N/Y/Y/Y/N/1200F 2 a) Appartement deux pièces, rue St Pierre.

Troisième étage dans immeuble neuf. Chauffage central, balcon sud. 5.000F par mois. b) Charmant studio près du centre-ville. 40 mètres carrés (= 40 square metres) au rez-de-chaussée, balcon donne sur le parc. 2.500F, charges comprises. 3 Je cherche un appartement à louer pour deux personnes en juin./Pour deux semaines./Le loyer, c'est combien?/Est-ce qu'il y a une machine à laver?/Puis-je voir l'appartement aujourd'hui?

58 1 Wrong in a) 1 roast chicken, 1 tea; Wrong in b) 2 chicken in wine, 1 cake, 2 black coffees, 1 brandy 2 a) l'addition; b) mangé; c) cognac; d) tout de suite; e) délicieux; f) moules 3 Oui, le poulet était délicieux./Mais il y a une erreur sur l'addition./Vous avez mis cinquante-cinq francs pour le steak mais sur la carte c'était quarante-cinq./Ce n'est pas grave./Deux cafés et un cognac, s'il vous plaît.

59 1 a) Christmas; b) 4; c) Dec 23rd; d) 3500F; e) half board 2 a) lisais; b) avons déménagé; c) avais/étais; d) regardait; e) suis sorti(e).

60 A 1) J'ai réservé une chambre. 2) Nous avons pris l'autoroute. 3) Nous sommes arrivé(e)s à 7h30. 4) Marc a stationné la voiture. 5) Je suis entré(e) dans l'hôtel. B 1) Je lisais mon journal. 2) Jean avait envie d'aller à Paris. 3) Je travaillais comme journaliste. 4) Ils avaient peur du tunnel. 5) C'était délicieux. C 1 Je réserverai une chambre. 2) Nous prendrons l'autoroute. 3) Nous arriverons à 7h30. 4) Marc stationnera la voiture. 5) J'entrerai dans l'hôtel. D 1) la mer bleue; 2) une salade verte; 3) un train direct; 4) du poulet rôti. 1) un petit garçon; 2) une jeune femme; 3) les vieilles villes; 4) le prochain train.

Verb Tables

Regular verbs

-ER Verbs	-RE Verbs	-IR Verbs
Donner	*Descendre*	*Finir*

Present Tense

-ER Verbs	-RE Verbs	-IR Verbs
Je donne	Je descends	Je finis
Tu donnes	Tu descends	Tu finis
Il/Elle donne	Il/Elle descend	Il/Elle finit
Nous donnons	Nous descendons	Nous finissons
Vous donnez	Vous descendez	Vous finissez
Ils/Elles donnent	Ils/Elles descendent	Ils/Elles finissent

Future tense

-ER Verbs	-RE Verbs	-IR Verbs
Je donnerai	Je descendrai	Je finirai
Tu donneras	Tu descendras	Tu finiras
Il/Elle donnera	Il/Elle descendra	Il/Elle finira
Nous donnerons	Nous descendrons	Nous finirons
Vous donnerez	Vous descendrez	Vous finirez
Ils/Elles donneront	Ils/Elles descendront	Ils/Elles finiront

Imperfect tense

-ER Verbs	-RE Verbs	-IR Verbs
Je donnais	Je descendais	Je finissais
Tu donnais	Tu descendais	Tu finissais
Il/Elle donnait	Il/Elle descendait	Il/Elle finissait
Nous donnions	Nous descendions	Nous finissions
Vous donniez	Vous descendiez	Vous finissiez
Ils/Elles donnaient	Ils/Elles descendaient	Ils/Elles finissaient

Past participle (for perfect tense)

-ER Verbs	-RE Verbs	-IR Verbs
donné	descendu	fini

Irregular verbs

	Aller	Avoir	Devoir	Dire	Ecrire	Etre	Faire
Present tense							
Je (J')	vais	ai	dois	dis	écris	suis	fais
Tu	vas	as	dois	dis	écris	es	fais
Il/Elle	va	a	doit	dit	écrit	est	fait
Nous	allons	avons	devons	disons	écrivons	sommes	faisons
Vous	allez	avez	devez	dites	écrivez	êtes	faites
Ils/Elles	vont	ont	doivent	disent	écrivent	sont	font
Future tense							
Je (J')	irai	aurai	devrai	dirai	écrirai	serai	ferai

(For other persons – **tu**, **il**, etc., the beginning of each verb – the stem –
is the same as for **Je**. Just add the appropriate ending.)

Je (J') allais avais devais disais écrivais étais faisais
(For the remaining persons just add the appropriate endings to the stem.)

Past participle (for perfect tense)

allé eu dû dit écrit été fait

	Mettre	*Pouvoir*	*Prendre*	*Venir*	*Voir*	*Vouloir*
Present tense						
Je	mets	peux	prends	viens	vois	veux
Tu	mets	peux	prends	viens	vois	veux
Il/Elle	met	peut	prend	vient	voit	veut
Nous	mettons	pouvons	prenons	venons	voyons	voulons
Vous	mettez	pouvez	prenez	venez	voyez	voulez
Ils/Elles	mettent	peuvent	prennent	viennent	voient	veulent

Future tense

Je mettrai pourrai prendrai viendrai verrai voudrai
(For the the remaining persons, just add the appropriate endings to the stem.)

Imperfect tense

Je mettais pouvais prenais venais voyais voulais
(For the the remaining persons, just add the appropriate endings to the stem.)

Past participle (for perfect tense)

mis pu pris venu vu voulu

Formation of the perfect tense

The present tense of **AVOIR** or **ETRE** + the past participle. Verbs forming the perfect tense with **ETRE**: **aller, arriver, descendre, entrer, monter, mourir, naître, partir, rester, retourner, sortir, tomber, venir** and verbs made from these, e.g. **devenir** – to become, **rentrer** – to come back. Also *all reflexive verbs.*

Formation of the future tense

Add the present tense endings of **AVOIR** to the final **-r** of the infinitive.
Je donner*ai*, tu finir*as*, il vendr*a*, etc.
Exceptions: **Je serai** – 'I will be', **j'aurai** – 'I will have', **je ferai** – 'I will do/make', **je viendrai** – 'I will come', **j'irai**, 'I will go'.

Formation of the imperfect tense

Remove the **-ons** ending from the present tense and add **-ais, -ais, -ait, -ions, -iez, -aient**.
Nous **parl-ons** **Je parlais, tu parlais, il parlait, nous parlions,** etc.

Vocabulary

Nouns – Gender is shown with (m) or (f) to show masculine or feminine gender.

Adjectives – Appear in masculine singular form only, except where feminine or plural forms are irregular.

Verbs appear in their infinitive form. Refer to pages 131–2 for the tenses of irregular verbs.

Abbreviations – (m) masculine; (f) feminine; (pl) plural; (irreg) irregular; * forms perfect tense with **être**; (pp) past participle.

A à at, to
abricot (m) apricot
accepter to accept
acheter to buy
addition (f) bill (in restaurant)
adorer to adore
adresse (f) address
adulte (m/f) adult
aéroport (m) airport
âge (m) age
agenda (m) appointments diary
agneau (m) lamb
agréable pleasant
aider to help
ail (m) garlic
aimable kind
aimer to like, to love
aîné elder
allemand German
Allemagne (f) Germany
aller* (irreg) to go; **Ça va** (That's) all right; **Ça va?** OK? All right? How are you?; **On y va?** Shall we go? **aller simple** (m) single ticket; **aller-retour** (m) return ticket
Allez la France! Come on France!
Allô! Hello? (on telephone)
alors well, then, so
Alpes (f. pl) Alps
alsacien Alsatian, from Alsace
américain American
Amérique (f) America
an (m) year; **Jour de l'An** New Year's Day
ananas (m) pineapple
anchois (m) anchovy
anglais English
Angleterre (f) England
année (f) year
anniversaire (m) anniversary, birthday
annonce (f) announcement; **petites annonces** small ads
antiquaire (m) antique dealer
apéritif (m) aperitif
appartement (m) flat (US apartment)
appel (m) call
appeler to call

s'appeler to be called
appétit (m) appetite; **Bon appétit!** Enjoy your meal!
apporter to bring
après after
après-midi (m/f) afternoon
argent (m) money; silver
arrivée (f) arrival
arriver* to arrive
arrondissement (m) district of Paris
ascenseur (m) lift (US elevator)
s'asseoir* (irreg) (pp **assis**) to sit down
assez enough, quite, fairly
assurance (f) insurance
astuce (f) trick
attendre to wait
au revoir goodbye
au, aux to the, at the; (cooked/served) with
au fond de at the end of
au moins at least
au-dessus de above
aujourd'hui today
aussi also, too
auteur (m) author
automobile (f) car, automobile
autonome autonomous
autoroute (f) motorway
autre other
avancer to advance, move forward
avant before
avec with
averse (f) shower (of rain)
avion (m) plane
avis (m) notice; advice, opinion; **A mon avis** In my opinion
avril April

B

bagages (m. pl) baggage, luggage
bain (m) bath
balcon (m) balcony
barré blocked, closed off
banque (f) bank
baskets (m. pl) trainers, tennis shoes
beau (f **belle**) beautiful, handsome, fine; **il fait beau** the weather's fine

beaux-arts (m) fine arts
beaucoup (de) much, many, a lot (of)
belge Belgian
Belgique (f) Belgium
bibliothèque (f) library
bien well; **bien sûr** of course
bière (f) beer
billet (m) ticket
bistro(t) (m) pavement café
blanc (f **blanche**) white
bleu blue
blond blond, light
blue-jean (m) jeans
boire (irreg) to drink
boisson (f) drink
boîte (f) tin, can, box
bon (f **bonne**) good; **Je suis dans la bonne queue?** Am I in the right queue? **Ah bon?** Really?
Bonjour Good morning/afternoon
Bonsoir Good evening
bord (m) edge, side
bordelais from Bordeaux
boulangerie (f) baker's shop
Bourgogne (f) Burgundy
bouteille (f) bottle
Bretagne (f) Brittany
breton (f **bretonne**) Breton, from Brittany
bricolage (m) do-it-yourself
bricoleur (f **bricoleuse**) handyman/handy-woman
brouillard (m) fog; **il fait du brouillard** it's foggy
brun brown
bureau de change currency exchange office; **bureau de location** rental office; **bureau de poste** post office

C
ça that; **Ça va?** How are you? Are you all right? (informal)
cadeau (m) present
cadet (f **cadette**) younger
café (m) café; **café-crème**, **café au lait** white coffee; **café-tabac** café-tobacconist's
caisse (f) till, cash-desk
calme calm
canard (m) duck
capitale (f) capital
capot (m) (car) bonnet
car (m) coach
carafe (f) carafe, jug
carnet (m) notebook; (of tickets) booklet
carotte (f) carrot
carte (f) card, menu; **carte de crédit** credit card; **carte des vins** wine list; **carte d'embarquement** boarding pass; **carte postale** postcard
ce (f **cette**) this, that; **ces** these, those
celui-ci/là (f **celle-ci/là**) this/that one; **ceux-ci/là** (f **celles-ci/là**) these/those (ones)
centime (m) centime (one-hundredth of a franc)
centre-ville (m) town centre
certainement certainly
chambre (f) (bed)room
champignon (m) mushroom
chance (f) luck; **Quelle chance!** What luck!
changer to change
chaque each, every
charcuterie (f) delicatessen
charges (f. pl) maintenance charges
charmant charming
chaud warm, hot (weather); **il fait chaud** it's warm/hot
chauffage (m) heating
chemin de fer (m) railway
chemise (f) shirt
chemisier (m) blouse
chèque (m) cheque; **chèque de voyage** traveller's cheque
cher (f **chère**) dear
chercher to look for
chéri darling
cheveux (m. pl) hair
chèvre (f) goat
chez at (home or work)
chiffre (m) figure, number
chocolat (m) chocolate
choisir to choose
chômage (m) unemployment
chose (f) thing; **autre chose?** anything else? **quelque chose** something
ciel (m) sky
circuler to circulate, to move around; **Allez, circulez!** Keep moving!
cirque (m) circus
citadelle (f) citadel
citron (m) lemon
clair clear, bright
clé (f) key; **fermé à clé** locked
climat (m) climate
coca (m) coca cola
combien how much, how many
comble (m) extreme, limit; **C'est le comble!** That's the last straw!
comme like, as
comment how; **Comment?** What? **Comment est-il?** What's he/it like?

Communauté Européenne (f) European Community
compagnie (f) company
compliqué complicated
composer to compose; (telephone) to dial
comprendre (irreg. see **prendre**) to understand
comprimé (m) tablet
compris understood; included
compte (m) account
comptoir (m) counter
conducteur (m) (f **conductrice**) driver
confirmer to confirm
connaître (irreg. pp **connu**) to know
coq au vin (m) chicken wine casserole
correspondance (f) correspondence; (train) connection
costume (m) suit, costume
côté (m) side; **à côté de** next to; **de l'autre côté** on the other side
côte (f) coast; **La Côte d'Azur** The Côte d'Azur (French Riviera)
couleur (f) colour
couloir (m) corridor
cours (m) exchange rate
court short
cousin (f **cousine**) cousin
coûter to cost
cravate (f) tie
crème (m) white coffee
crêpe (f) pancake
croire (irreg. pp **cru**) to believe
croque-monsieur (m) toasted cheese and ham sandwich
crudités (f. pl) dish of raw vegetables
cuisine (f) kitchen; cooking, cuisine
cuit cooked; **bien cuit** well cooked

D **d'abord** at first
d'accord all right, agreed
dans in
danser to dance
de of, from
décembre (m) December
décider to decide
décrocher to take off the (telephone) receiver
défense de stationner (f) no parking
degré (m) degree
déjeuner (m) lunch; **petit déjeuner** breakfast
délicieux (f. **délicieuse**) delicious
demain tomorrow; **à demain** till tomorrow
déménager to move (house)

demi half; **demi-douzaine** (**de**) (f) half-dozen; **demi-pension** half-board; **faire demi-tour** to reverse (in car)
dent (f) tooth; **mal aux dents** toothache
dépannage (m) breakdown
départ (m) departure
département (m) French administrative district; **route départementale** (f) minor road
dépendre (**de**) to depend (on); **Ça dépend** That depends
depuis since, for
dernier (f **dernière**) last; latest
derrière behind
descendre* to go down; (vehicle) to get off
désirer to want, to wish
désolé sorry
détester to hate, to detest
devant in front of
devoir (irreg. pp **dû**) to have to, must
différence (f) difference
difficile difficult
digestif (m) after-dinner liqueur
dimanche (m) Sunday
dire (irreg. pp **dit**) to say, to tell
direction (f) direction; management
discothèque (f) discotheque
disque de stationnement (m) parking disc
divorcé divorced
dommage (m) pity
donner to give; **donner sur** to look out on to
dos (m) back; **mal au dos** backache
douche (f) shower
Douvres (m) Dover
doux (f **douce**) mild; sweet; **il fait doux** the weather is mild
douzaine (f) dozen
droit straight; **tout droit** straight on
droite (f) right; **à droite** on the right

E
eau (f) water
éclaircie (f) bright period
écossais Scottish
Ecosse (f) Scotland
écouter to listen (to)
écrire (irreg. pp **écrit**) to write
s'écrire to be spelt; **Comment ça s'écrit?** How do you spell it?
édition (f) edition
effet (m) effect; **en effet** indeed, quite right
église (f) church
eh bien well
élégant smart, elegant
elle she, it

embarquement (m) boarding; **carte d'embarquement** (f) boarding pass
embrayage (m) clutch (in car)
emporter to take away
en in
en attendant whilst waiting
encaisser to cash
enchanté delighted, pleased to meet you
énergique energetic
en face (de) opposite
enfance (f) childhood
enfant (m/f) child; **menu enfants** children's menu
enlever to take off, to take away
enregistrer to record; (luggage) to check in
ensemble together
entrecôte (f) entrecote, rib steak
entrée (f) starter course
entreprise (f) company
entrer* to enter
envie desire, intention; **avoir envie (de)** to feel like
envoyer (irreg future **j'enverrai**) to send
épeler to spell
équipé equipped; **cuisine équipée** fitted kitchen
équitation (f) horse riding
erreur (f) error, mistake
escargot (m) snail
Espagne (f) Spain
espérer to hope
essayer to try; **salon d'essayage** (m) fitting room
essence (f) petrol; **station d'essence** (f) petrol station
est (m) East
est-ce que is it that (in questions)
estimer to estimate, to assess
et and
étage (m) floor, storey; **au premier étage** on the first floor
Etats-Unis (m. pl) United States
été (m) summer; **en été** in summer
étrange strange
étranger (f **étrangère**) stranger; foreigner; **à l'étranger** abroad
être (irreg. pp **été**) to be
étude (f) study
étudiant/e (m/f) student
eurochèque (m) Eurocheque
européen (f **européenne**) European
excuser to excuse; **Excusez-moi!** Excuse me, sorry
exemple (m) **par exemple** for example

exister to exist
expliquer to explain
express (m) (drink) black coffee; (train) express
exquis exquisite
extrêmement extremely

F

fabrication (f) manufacture
fabriquer to manufacture
faire (irreg. pp **fait**) to do, to make; **au fait** informed, knowledgeable
familial of the family; **une familiale** an estate car
famille (f) family
farci stuffed
faut (irreg. present of **falloir**); **il faut** it is necessary
femme (f) woman; wife
fermé shut, closed
fermer to shut, to close
fête (f) festival, public holiday; **Fête du Travail** (f) May Day, Labour Day
feuille de maladie (f) sickness certificate
feux (m. pl) (traffic) lights; **feux d'artifice** fireworks
fiche (f) form; **fiche voyageur** hotel registration form
fier (f **fière**) proud
fièvre (f) fever
filet (m) fillet steak
fille (f) girl; daughter
fils (m) son
finalement finally, at last, in the end
finir to finish
flegmatique phlegmatic
fois (f) time, occasion
folklorique folk; **concert folklorique** folk concert
fond (m) end, back, bottom
fraise (f) strawberry
franc (m) franc
français French
fréquent frequent
frère (m) brother
frit fried
froid cold; (weather) **il fait froid** it's cold
fromage (m) cheese
fruit(s) (m. pl) fruit; **fruits de mer** shellfish
fumé smoked
fumeur (m) smoker

G

galette (f) savoury pancake
garçon (m) boy; waiter
gare (f) station; **gare SNCF** rail station

garni garnished
gauche (f) left; **à gauche** on the left
gentil (f **gentille**) nice, kind
gîte (m) rented farmhouse
glace (f) ice cream
gorge (f) throat; **mal à la gorge** a sore throat
goûter to taste
grand big, large; (people) tall
grand-chose (in negatives) **pas grand-chose** not much
grand lit (m) double bed
grand-mère (f) grandmother
grave grave, serious
grenoblois from Grenoble
grenouille (f) frog
grippe (f) influenza
gris grey
guichet (m) counter, ticket office
guitare (f) guitar
gymnastique (f) gymnastics

H

habillé dressed
habiter to live
haricot (m) French bean
hein? eh? right?
hésiter to hesitate
heure (f) hour, time of day; o'clock; **Quelle heure est-il?** What time is it? **Il est dix heures** It's ten o'clock
hier yesterday
histoire (f) story, history
hiver (m) winter; **en hiver** in winter
homme (m) man
horizontalement horizontally
horreur (f) horror; **J'ai horreur de** I hate
hôtel (m) hotel
huile (f) oil
huitante eighty (in Belgium and Switzerland)

I

ici here
idée (f) idea
identité (f) identity; **pièce d'identité** identity document
il y a there is/are; ago
illimité unlimited
illustré (m) magazine
imaginer to imagine
immatriculation (f) (vehicle) registration
immeuble (m) building
importer to import
indicatif (m) (telephone) code
indiscipliné undisciplined

individualiste individualistic
industrie (f) industry
industriel (f **industrielle**) industrial
ingénieur (m) engineer
s'inquiéter to worry
insister to insist
interdit forbidden
intéressant interesting
intéresser to interest
intermittent intermittent
Italie (f) Italy
italien (f **italienne**) Italian

J

jambon (m) ham
janvier (m) January
Japon (m) Japan
japonais Japanese
jardin (m) garden
jardinage (m) gardening
jardinier (m) gardener
jaune yellow
je I
jeudi (m) Thursday
jeune young
joli pretty
jouer to play
jour (m) day; **Le Jour de l'An** New Year's Day
journal (m) newspaper
journée (f) day; **Bonne journée!** Have a good day!
juin (m) June
jupe (f) skirt
jus d'orange (m) orange juice
jusqu'à as far as; until
juste just

K

kilométrage (m) (car) mileage
kilomètre (m) kilometre

L

la, l' the (f); her, it
là there
là-bas over there
laisser to leave
lait (m) milk
langue (f) tongue; language
lavabo (m) washbasin
lave-vaisselle (m) dishwasher
le, l' the (m); him, it
légume (m) vegetable
lequel (f **laquelle**) which (one); **lesquels** (f **lesquelles**) which (ones)
les the (pl); them
lettre (f) letter

leur their
librairie (f) bookshop
libre free; **libre-service** self-service
limonade (f) lemonade
lire (irreg. pp **lu**) to read
lit (m) bed
livre (f) pound
livre (m) book
loin far
loisirs (m. pl) hobbies, leisure activities;
  centre de loisirs (m) leisure centre
Londres (m) London
long (f **longue**) long
longtemps a long time
louer to hire, to rent
lourd heavy
loyer (m) rent
lundi (m) Monday
lunettes (f. pl) spectacles
lyonnais from Lyon

M **machine à laver** (f) washing machine
madame (f) Madam; Mrs
mademoiselle (f) Miss
magasin (m) shop; **grand magasin**
  department store
magnifique magnificent
mai (m) May
mairie (f) town hall
mais but
maison (f) house; **à la maison** (at) home
mal badly; **pas mal** not bad; **J'ai mal** I've a
  pain; **mal de mer** (m) sea-sickness
malade ill
maladie (f) illness
maman (m) Mother, Mummy
manger to eat
manquer to miss; to lack; **il ne manque
  pas de** there's no lack of
manuel (m) manual
marché (m) market
marcher (people) to walk; (machines) to
  function, to work
mardi (m) Tuesday
mari (m) husband
marié married
marionnette (f) puppet
marque (f) make, brand
marseillais from Marseille; **La
  Marseillaise** the French National
  Anthem
matin (m) morning
matinée (f) morning (of activities)
mauvais bad

maximum (m) maximum
Méditerranée (f) the Mediterranean
meilleur better, best
même even; same; (on telephone) **C'est
  lui-/elle-même** Speaking
mémoire (f) memory
mer (f) sea
merci thank you
mercredi (m) Wednesday
mère (f) mother
mes my (pl)
Messieurs-dames Ladies and
  gentlemen
météo (f) weather forecast
mètre (m) metre
mettre (irreg. pp **mis**) to put
midi (m) midday; **Le Midi** the southern
  half of France
mieux better, best; **aller mieux** to feel
  better
mil (in dates) (one) thousand
mille thousand
mince slim
minéral mineral
minuit (m) midnight
mixte mixed
modèle (m) (car) model
modéré moderate
moi me
moins less, least
mois (m) month
moitié (f) half
moment (m) moment; **en ce moment** at
  the moment
mon (f **ma**, pl **mes**) my
monnaie (f) small change
monsieur Sir, Mr
monsieur-dame Sir, Madam
montagne (f) mountain
monter* to climb, to go up
montre (f) wristwatch
morceau (m) piece
mot (m) word; **mots croisés** crossword
moules marinière (f. pl) mussels in wine
mourir* (irreg. pp **mort**) to die
mousse (f) (dessert) mousse
musée (m) museum
musique (f) music

N **nager** to swim
naissance (f) birth
naître* (irreg. pp **né**) to be born
natal native; **ma ville natale** my home
  town

nationalité (f) nationality
nature (coffee) black
ne ... pas not; **ne ... aucun** not any; **ne
... jamais** never; **ne ... personne** no
one; **ne ... plus** no more/longer; **ne ...
rien** nothing
neiger to snow; **il neige** it's snowing
neuf (f **neuve**) (brand-)new
niçois from Nice
Noël (m) Christmas
noir black
nom (m) name, surname
non no; **moi non plus** me neither
nonante ninety (in Belgium and
Switzerland)
nord North
normand Norman, from Normandy
Normandie (f) Normandy
noté noted
notre (pl **nos**) our
nous we, us
nouveau (f **nouvelle**) new
nuage (m) cloud
nuit (f) night
numéro (m) number

O **occasion** (f) bargain; opportunity
œuf (m) egg
office de tourisme (f) tourist office
offre (f) offer
offrir (irreg. pp **offert)** to offer, to give;
C'est pour offrir? Is it for a gift?
Oh là là! Wow! Gosh! Oh dear!
oignon (m) onion
olive (f) olive
on dit que ... One says/They say that ...
orage (m) storm
orange pressée (f) freshly squeezed
orange juice
ordinaire ordinary
ordinateur (m) computer
où where; **d'où** from where
ou or; **Ou ... ou** Either ... or
ouest (m) West
oui yes
ouvert open
ouvrir (irreg. pp **ouvert**) to open

P **panier** (m) basket
panne (f) breakdown; **en panne** broken
down, out of order
pantalon (m) (pair of) trousers
Pâques (m) Easter
paquet (m) packet

par by; per; through; **par exemple** for
example
paraître (irreg. pp **paru**) to appear
pardon pardon, excuse me
paresseux (f **paresseuse**) lazy
parfait perfect
parisien (f **parisienne**) Parisian
parler to speak
part (f) part; **à part** apart, separate(ly)
partager to share
partir* (irreg) to leave, to depart; **à partir
de** (starting) from
partout everywhere
pas not; **pas de** not any
passage interdit (m) No through road
passager (m) (f **passagère**) passenger
passeport (m) passport
passer* to go over/across
passer to pass/spend (time)
pâté de foie gras (m) rich liver pâté
patienter to wait, to be patient
pâtisserie (f) cake-shop
payer to pay
pays (m) country; region
paysage (m) scenery, landscape
pendant during
penser to think
Pentecôte (f) Whitsun
père (m) father
permis de conduire (m) driving licence
personne (f) person; **par personne** per
person
petit little, small; short
peu (de) little (of)
peur (f) fear; **avoir peur de** to be afraid of
peut-être perhaps, maybe
pharmacie (f) chemist's (US drug-store)
pharmacien chemist (US druggist)
Picardie (f) Picardy
pièce d'identité (f) identity document
pièce (f) coin; room; (spare) part; **10F la
pièce** 10 francs each
pied (m) foot
pilule (f) pill
pimenté hot, spicy
piscine (f) swimming pool
place (f) town square; place, seat
plage (f) beach
plaire (irreg. pp **plu**) to please; **s'il vous
plaît** please
plaisanter to joke
plat (m) (food) dish, course
plateau (m) tray
plein full; **Faites le plein!** (petrol) Fill up!

en plein centre right in the centre
pleuvoir (irreg. pp **plu**) to rain; **Il pleut** It's raining
plomb (m) lead
plongeur (f **plongeuse**) washer-up
plus more, most; **moi non plus** me neither
plusieurs several
plutôt rather
pneu (m) tyre
pois (m) pea
poisson (m) fish
pollué polluted
pomme (f) apple
pommes frites chips (US French fries)
porte (f) door, gate
porter to carry; to wear
Portugal (m) Portugal
poste restante (f) (post office) mail collection counter
poulet (m) chicken
pour for
pourquoi why
pouvoir (irreg. pp **pu**) to be able, can
préférer to prefer
premier (f **première**) first
prendre (irreg. pp **pris**) to take; (food and drink) to have
prénom (m) Christian/first name
près (**de**) near (to)
présenter to introduce **se présenter** to introduce oneself; **Je vous présente** … Let me introduce…
presque nearly, almost
presse (f) press (newspapers)
pression (f) draught beer
prêt ready
prévu expected, scheduled
prier to request; **Je vous en prie** Don't mention it, please do
principal main
printemps (m) spring; **au printemps** in spring
privé private
prix (m) price
problème (m) problem
prochain next
professeur (m) teacher
programme (m) programme; **programme des spectacles** diary of events
promenade (f) walk, stroll
se promener to go for a walk
promotion (f) promotional offer; **en promotion** on special offer

propos: à propos by the way
proposer to suggest, to offer
propriétaire (m/f) owner, proprietor
provençal from Provence
publier to publish
puis then
puis-je? may I? can I?
puisque since, as
Pyrénées (f. pl) Pyrenees

Q

quai (m) (railway) platform
quand when; **quand même** even so
quart (m) quarter
quartier (m) quarter, district (of town); **quartier latin** Latin Quarter (of Paris)
que that, which, whom
quel (f **quelle**) which, what (a). **Quel dommage!** What a pity! **Quelle chance!** What luck!
quelque some; **quelque chose** something; **quelqu'un** someone
Qu'est-ce que What? (object). **Qu'est-ce qui?** What? (subject). **Qu'est-ce que c'est?** What is it? **Qu'est-ce qui ne va pas?** What's the matter?
qui that, which, who
quitter to leave

R

raisonnable reasonable
rapide rapid, fast
rapide (m) express train
ravi delighted
recette (f) recipe
recevoir (irreg. pp **reçu**) to receive
réduit reduced
regarder to watch, to look at
région (f) region
régional regional
registre (m) register
regretter to regret
remède (m) remedy
remercier to thank; **Je vous remercie** Thank you
remplir to fill, (forms) to fill out
rencontrer to meet
rendez-vous (m) meeting
renseignements (m. pl) information
rentrée (f) return to work/school
rentrer* to go/come back (home)
réparer to repair
repas (m) meal
repasser to call in again
répéter to repeat

réservation (f) reservation
réserver to reserve, to book
rester* to stay, to remain
retard (m) late(ness); **être en retard** to be late
retirer (money) to withdraw
retour (m) return; **aller-retour** (m) return ticket
retourner* to return, to go back
revenir* (irreg. pp **revenu**) to come back; **Ça revient moins cher** It works out cheaper
revue (f) magazine
rez-de-chaussée (m) ground floor (US first floor)
rien nothing; **de rien** don't mention it
risque (m) risk; (car insurance) **tous risques** comprehensive
riz (m) rice
robe (f) dress
rose pink
rôti roast
rouge red
route (f) road; **route nationale** major road; **route départementale** minor road
routier (f **routière**): **gare routière** (f) bus/coach station
rue (f) street, road (in town)

S **saison** (f) season
salade (f) salad
salle (f) room; **salle à manger** dining room; **salle de bains** bathroom; **salle de séjour** living room
salon (m) living room; **salon d'essayage** fitting room
Salut! Hello! Hi! (informal)
samedi (m) Saturday
sans without
sauf except
savoir (irreg. pp **su**) to know (fact)
seconde (f) second
secrétaire (m/f) secretary
semaine (f) week
sens unique (m) one-way street
séparé separated
septante seventy (in Belgium and Switzerland)
sérieux (f **sérieuse**) serious
service (m) service; **service (non) compris** service (not) included
seul alone; **une seule nuit** only/just one night
seulement only

si if
signer to sign
s'il vous plaît please
simple simple; **un aller simple** a single ticket
ski (m) skiing; **faire du ski** to go skiing
société (f) company
sœur (f) sister
soir (m) evening
sole (f) (fish) sole
soleil (m) sun
somme (f) (money) sum, amount
son (f **sa**, pl **ses**) his/her
sortie (f) exit
sortir* (irreg) to go out, to exit
soupe (f) soup
sous under; **sous-sol** (m) basement
souvenir (m) souvenir, memory
se souvenir (de) (irreg. pp **souvenu**) to remember
spécial special
spectacle (m) entertainment
station d'essence (f) petrol (US gas) station; **station de ski** ski resort; **station de taxis** taxi rank
stationner to park
steak-frites (m) steak and chips (US French fries)
studio (m) bed-sit, one-room apartment
sucre (m) sugar
sud (m) South
suffire (irreg. pp **suffi**) to suffice, to be enough
Suisse (f) Switzerland
suisse Swiss
suivre (irreg. pp **suivi**) to follow
super (fuel) 4-star, high octane
supermarché (m) supermarket
supplément (m) supplement, (menu) **en supplément** extra
sur on
surtout above all, especially
sympathique (people) likeable, nice
symptôme (m) symptom
syndicat d'initiative (m) tourist information office

T

taille (f) size; waist
tant (de) so much, so many
tard late
tarif (m) rate, price, fare
tarte (f) tart
tee-shirt (m) T-shirt
télécarte (f) telephone card

téléphone (m) telephone
téléphoner to telephone
téléviseur (m) television (set)
tellement so much; pas tellement not all
that much
température (f) temperature
temps (m) time; weather; de temps en
temps from time to time
terminer to finish
terrasse (f) terrace
tête (f) head; mal à la tête headache; tête
de veau brawn
thé (m) tea
timbre (m) (postage) stamp
toi you (familiar)
tomber* to fall
ton (f ta, pl tes) your (familiar)
tonalité (f) (dialling) tone
tour (f) tower; La Tour Eiffel The Eiffel
Tower
touristique tourist's; menu touristique
basic menu
tourner to turn
tout (m. pl tous) all; tout de suite
immediately; tout droit straight on; pas
du tout not at all
trafic (m) traffic
train (m) train; train à grande vitesse
(TGV) TGV high-speed train; train
express fast train; train omnibus local
(slow) train
tranche (f) slice
tranquille quiet, peaceful
travail (m) work; Fête du Travail (f) May
Day, Labour Day
travailler to work
travailleur (f travailleuse) hard-working
très very
trouver to find
se trouver to be situated
tu you (familiar)
tunnel (m) tunnel; Le Tunnel sous la
Manche The Channel Tunnel

U un, une a; one
Union Européenne (f) European Union
uniquement only, solely
université (f) university

V vacances (f. pl) holidays; en vacances on
holiday
valable valid
valeur (f) value

valise (f) suitcase
valoir (irreg. pp valu) to be worth; il vaut
mieux ... You'd better ...
véhicule (m) vehicle
vélo (m) bicycle
venir* (irreg. pp venu) to come; venir de
to have just
vent (m) wind; il fait du vent it's windy
ventre (m) stomach; mal au ventre
stomach ache
vérifer to check
verre (m) glass; verres de contact
contact lenses
vers towards; (time) about
vert green; carte verte green (motor
insurance) card
verticalement vertically
vieux (f vieille) old
ville (f) town, city
vin (m) wine
visite (f) visit
visiter to visit (a place)
vite quickly
vitesse (f) speed
vitrine (f) shop window
vive la France! Long live France!
vocabulaire (m) vocabulary
voici here is
voie (f) way
voilà here is/are, there is/are
voir (irreg. pp vu) to see; Voyons Let's
see
voiture (f) car
vol (m) flight
votre (pl vos) your (formal)
vouloir (irreg. pp voulu) to want
vous you
voyage (m) journey; Bon voyage! Have a
good journey!
voyager to travel

W wagon-restaurant (m) restaurant car
WC (m. pl) toilets

Y y there; y compris including
yeux (m. pl) eyes

Z zéro zero
zone (f) zone, area; zone bleue blue
(restricted parking) zone; zone piétonne pedestrian area
zut! damn! blast!

Language and Topic Indexes

Numbers refer to units.
Numbers in bold type indicate that an irregular verb is recorded at the end of the unit.

LANGUAGE

Accents 14
Adjectives:
  agreement 1
  position 12
  possessive 5, 18 40
  of colour 32
  petit, grand 41
  beau, nouveau, vieux, blanc
    49, 56, 57
Adverbs 28
Age 17
ALLER **26**, 43, 50
Alphabet 27
Articles:
  indefinite *un, une* 2
  definite *le/la/l'/les* 6, 9
au, à la, à l', aux 14, 22
AVOIR 6, 17, **25**, 33, 46, 59
ce, cette, ces 15
celui, celle, ceux, celles 20
comment, quoi, pardon 47
Comparisons – more/less
  23, 36
Countries 21, 24
Days, dates, months, seasons
  9, 27, 40
depuis 17
Describing people 41
DEVOIR **54**
DIRE **52**
du, de la, de l', des 14, 22
ECRIRE **45**
est-ce que 6
ETRE 18, **25**
FAIRE **29**, 30
hein? 20
il faut 18, 35
il y a 6, 39
JOUER (*à/de*) 29
lequel, laquelle, lesquels,
  lesquelles 20
Let's 52
METTRE **50**, 58
mil, mille 52
moi 22, 54

moins 23, 36
Negatives 10, 39, 42, 46
n'est-ce pas? 20
Nouns:
  gender 1, 2, 35
  plural 3, 26
Numbers:
  zero 16
  1—29 4
  30—60 8
  70—100 16
  hundreds 11
  thousands 20, 52
  ordinal numbers 28, 51
  handwritten 16
  telephone 16
Object pronouns:
  le, la, les 15
  en 43, 44
  position 32
  y 53
On 38, 39
Ou … ou 51
Past participles 34, 38, 58
PLEUVOIR 30
plus 23, 36
Points of the compass 24
PORTER 41
Possessive adjectives 5, 18,
  40
Possessive pronouns with *à*
  54
POUVOIR 45, **47**
Pronunciation 3, 4, 6, 14, 19,
  24, 48
Quantity (expressions of) 8,
  47
quel, quelle 20, 31
quelque chose 23
qu'est-ce que/qui? 31, 33
se 24, 53
Telephone numbers 16, 50
Time of day 4, 28
tu and *vous* 25, 28, 46
VENIR **30**
Venir de 30
Verbs:
  Present tense -*ER* verbs
  5, 7, 12; -*IR* verbs 38; -*RE*
  verbs 43; with *depuis* 17
  Perfect tense 10, 38, 39,
    43, 53, 54, 58

Future tense 55, 57
Future with *aller* 26
Imperfect tense 53, 58, 59
Imperative 11, 22, 42, 43,
  52
Reflexive 24, 53
VOULOIR **51**
Weather 30, 36

TOPICS

Accommodation 57
Airport 55
Apologising 39
Banks, money 45
Café, restaurant 2, 10, 14,
  22, 26, 34, 38, 46, 58
Countries, regions, towns 21,
  24, 43
Crossing the Channel 59
Directions 6, 18
Entertainment 9
France:
  Paris 12
  regions, towns 24, 36
Franglais 41, 55
Greetings 1, 5, 25, 28, 49
Holidays 40
Hotels 3, 15, 16, 27, 39, 51
Illness, medicine 33
Motoring:
  Breakdown 35
  Car rental 23
  Insurance 52
  Parking 42
  Petrol 11
  Roads 47
  Speed limits 47
Newspapers 54
Post Office 21
Shopping:
  Books 56
  Clothes 32
  Food 8, 44
  Jewellery 20
Sports 29
Taxis 54
Telephone 26, 50
Time of day 4, 28
Trains 7, 19, 31
Weather 30, 36